RECYCLII
INTERMEDIATE
ENGLISH
REVISED EDITION

CLARE WEST

GEORGIAN PRESS

Georgian Press (Jersey) Limited
Pirouet House
Union Street
St Helier
Jersey JE4 8ZQ
Channel Islands

First published by Georgian Press (Jersey) Limited 1998
Reprinted 1998, 1999
This revised edition first published 2004

ISBN 1-873630-42-5 (without key)
ISBN 1-873630-43-3 (with key)

Produced by AMR Limited
Drawings by Art Construction and David Birdsall

Printed in Egypt by International Printing House

CONTENTS

SECTION 3   SITUATIONS

SECTION 4   WRITING

IRREGULAR VERBS

The Key begins on page 129 of the With Key edition.

INTRODUCTION

Recycling Intermediate English is for students at lower-intermediate to intermediate level who want to improve their general English. It also offers useful extra practice to those preparing for the Cambridge Preliminary English Test (PET). It can be used to supplement any coursebook at this level, and is suitable for use in the classroom, for homework, or (in the case of the With Key edition) for self-study.

The book aims to provide:

- coverage of the four main areas of difficulty at this level – grammar, vocabulary, situations and writing
- short, clear explanations and examples
- extensive practice of each point covered
- a simple, attractive layout, so that the material is easy to use.

Recycling Intermediate English is divided into four distinct sections:

Section 1 GRAMMAR (35 units)

This is the largest section of the book, covering all the major grammatical points at PET level.

Section 2 VOCABULARY (20 units)

This section presents and practises vocabulary from sixteen key PET topics.

Section 3 SITUATIONS (22 units)

This section covers a wide range of situations and functions needed at intermediate level, selected from the PET syllabus.

Section 4 WRITING (11 units)

This section offers clear guidance on a variety of different writing tasks, with model compositions, help with spelling, tips on writing techniques, and useful expressions to learn and practise.

RECYCLING units are an important element of this book. They occur in Sections 1 and 2 after every four units, to help students remember and practise new material. Previous items are recycled, not just those from the previous group of units.

How should the book be used?

Teachers using the book as supplementary material should feel free to dip in and out of units and sections as they wish. However, in Section 1 there is a progression of grammatical items from Units 1 to 35, so students studying on their own should work through the units in order. Recycling units are also best used in the correct sequence – for example, Unit 5 after Units 1–4.

Other books in the series

This book is part of a series by the same author, ranging from elementary to advanced.

Recycling Elementary English is for elementary students, and those preparing for the Cambridge Key English Test (KET).

Recycling Your English is for upper-intermediate students, and those preparing for the Cambridge First Certificate examination (FCE) or the IGCSE in ESL.

Recycling Advanced English is for advanced students, and those studying for the Cambridge Certificate in Advanced English (CAE) or the Certificate of Proficiency in English (CPE) examinations.

PARTS OF SPEECH

A VERB is a doing word, which describes an action or a state. It can be used in different tenses, depending on the time of the action:

- I **went** home.
- She**'ll see** you tomorrow.
- They **weren't** there.

The SUBJECT of a sentence usually comes before the verb:

- **The postman** always delivers the letters on time.

The OBJECT of a sentence usually comes after the verb:

- I found **the money** on the table.

A NOUN is a way of naming people, animals or objects. It can be uncountable, singular or plural:

- He gave us some helpful **information**.
- We found a **wallet** on the **pavement**.
- There were ten thousand **people** in the **crowd**.

SINGULAR means only one of something:

- **A** small **child** was sitting on the bench.

PLURAL means more than one of something:

- There were **five** beautiful Persian **carpets** for sale.

An ARTICLE is used before a singular noun.

Definite article: • I watched **the** sun go down.
Indefinite article: • We bought **a** new car last week.

A PRONOUN is used instead of a noun:

- **She** spent all her money.
- **They** were angry with the government.

An ADJECTIVE describes or modifies a noun, or is used with verbs like be or seem:

- a **delicious** meal
- He is **happy**.
- They seem **intelligent**.

An ADVERB describes or modifies verbs, or adjectives, or other adverbs:

- She danced very **gracefully**.
- I am **awfully** sorry.
- He drove **incredibly** fast.

A PREPOSITION is a word used before a noun or pronoun, to connect it to the rest of the sentence:

- He works **in** Glasgow.
- They live **by** the sea.
- She sat **near** the fire.

LINKING WORDS connect sentences or parts of sentences:

- She waited, **but** the bus didn't come.
- **As soon as** he arrived, they started their meal.

Present simple

The **present simple** is used to talk about regular or frequent actions, often with adverbs like **never, seldom, occasionally, sometimes, often, usually** and **always**:
• *Karen usually goes shopping on Saturdays.*

It is also used for facts that are always or usually true: • *Vincent comes from Paris.*

Note the common **-s/-es** ending after **he/she/it**: • *She laughs all the time.*

This is how you make the negative form, with **don't** and **doesn't**:
• *You don't cook as well as Bob.* • *She doesn't always seem to understand.*

This is how you make a question, with **do** and **does**:
• *Where do you keep your scissors?* • *Does he often say that?*

But notice: • *Who speaks Italian?* • *Who lives next door?*

A Complete the sentences, using one of the following verbs in the correct form:
*close   come   drink
drive   help   make
phone   rise   teach   tell*

1 You can see that the sun always _____ in the east.
2 She usually _____ the truth if she can.
3 The shops _____ at 5.30 p.m. most days.
4 Eva _____ from Latvia, I think.
5 My friend often _____ mistakes in her homework.
6 Mrs Logan _____ Italian to beginners.
7 Helga _____ a Mercedes, doesn't she?
8 Tim _____ his girlfriend every day when he's away.
9 I sometimes _____ my brother with his maths.
10 My grandparents _____ tea at least six times a day.

B Make the sentences into a question, starting with a question word.

1 Miho comes from – I don't know where.
2 You listen to BBC World Service, but I don't know when.
3 You sometimes lend James money, but I don't understand why.
4 Someone in the class speaks Spanish, but I don't know who.

Now make these sentences into a question, starting with *Do* or *Does*.

5 He pays his bills every three months.
6 Your friends agree with you.
7 His friends and relatives send him cards on his birthday.
8 I need to see the dentist twice a year.

C Make the sentences negative.

1 I work for a large company.
2 Pierre writes to his parents every week.
3 We often eat chocolate in the evening.
4 The old man always swims in the sea before lunch.
5 We believe what you say.
6 Daisy often rides her bike these days.

Present continuous

> The **present continuous** is used to talk about things happening now, often with adverbs like **now, at the moment, at present, today** and **this week**:
> • *Peter isn't here at the moment; he's doing the shopping.*
>
> It can also be used, with a future expression, to talk about the future:
> • *I'm seeing him tonight.*   • *Are you taking them to school tomorrow?*
>
> Note that the following verbs do **not** usually take the **continuous** form:
> • *believe, belong, contain, dislike, hate, impress, know, like, love, mean, need, owe, own, prefer, seem, suppose, surprise, understand, want, wish*

A Complete the sentences with the correct form of the verb in brackets.

1 Tony _____ a bath at the moment. (have)
2 It's very cold, isn't it? I think it _____ outside. (freeze)
3 Listen, everybody. Giuseppe _____ a story by Roald Dahl today. (read)
4 It's 8 o'clock in the morning and Mr Biggs _____ to work, as usual. (drive)
5 Jeanne _____ her new jeans, isn't she? (wear)
6 The trees _____ their leaves now that it's autumn. (lose)
7 The cat _____ its supper; it _____ some milk. (not eat, just drink)
8 Everybody _____ home from work now, and all the trains are crowded. (hurry)
9 Look! He _____ you how to mend it next time it breaks. (show)
10 At present Raschid _____ in Toronto. (study)

B There's a new girl in your class today. Ask her some questions about her future plans, using the present continuous of the verb in brackets.

1 How long _____ in this town / village / class / school? (you / stay)
2 Where _____ to study in future? (you / plan)
3 What _____ this evening/this weekend? (you / do)
4 What kind of job _____ to do? (you / hope)
5 Where _____ for your next holiday? (you / go)

C Some of these sentences are not correct. Tick (✔) the right ones, and correct the wrong ones.

1 I'm not understanding what the teacher said.
2 Is this dictionary belonging to you?
3 How are you feeling now?
4 What is this word meaning, please?
5 I'm needing a lot more information before I decide.
6 She's planning to visit Egypt next year.
7 We're hoping to buy a flat soon.
8 How much are you know about your family history?

There is, There are, It is

When you talk about something for the first time, use **There is/There are**:
- *There's a box on the table.*   • *Are there any museums in town?*

You can use an auxiliary (helping verb) and **be**:
- *There must be a bus strike.*   • *There will be trouble.*

If you have already mentioned something, use **it/they** to refer to it/them:
- *That's my car. It's a lot older than yours!*   • *The books? They're mine!*

A Complete the sentences, using *is there, there's, is it* or *it's*.

1 _____ a wonderful beach two kilometres away from the hotel.
2 Have you seen the Mr Bean film? _____ very funny!
3 _____ anybody waiting for this little girl?
4 Try using this key; I think _____ the right one.
5 I don't suppose _____ enough bread left to make a sandwich.
6 We could go to the Theatre Royal; _____ open this week?

B Complete the sentences, using *are there, there are, they're* or *are they*.

1 Don't look at anybody else's answers; _____ often wrong!
2 Some people are ill, so _____ only eight students in class today.
3 I know _____ several other employees who could do this job.
4 _____ any problems you need help with?
5 Those boys? Don't tell me _____ your friends!
6 Pass me those sweets; _____ yours?

It is used impersonally with adjectives, not referring to any particular thing:
- *It's difficult to give the right answer.*   • *It's nice of you to say that.*

C Decide whether to use *It's* or *There's* in these sentences.

1 ____ useful to have your own computer.
2 ____ no one at the bus stop.
3 ____ a cat sitting on the fence.
4 ____ a bus you could catch if you like.
5 ____ easy to make a mistake.
6 ____ not necessary to show your ticket.
7 ____ a café where we could meet.
8 ____ somebody on the phone for you.
9 ____ dangerous to run here.
10 ____ kind of her to help.
11 ____ very rude to shout.
12 ____ a lot of work to do.
13 ____ important not to fail.
14 ____ a ruined castle on the hill.
15 ____ pleasant sitting in the sun.
16 ____ not much time left.

UNIT 4

The future

The most common future form is the **present continuous** with a future expression (see **Unit 2**), and **going to**, both used for planned arrangements and intentions:
- *I'm writing letters tonight, so I can't come out.*   • *He's going to be an architect when he finishes his studies.*   • *She isn't going to marry him now.*
- *Are you going to book the flights?*

Will and **shall** should be used in these situations:
a predictions: • *I think she'll win the race.*
b instant decisions: • *It's hot in here; I'll open the window.*
c offers of help: • *Shall I help you with those files?*
d promises: • *I'll be very careful with the money!*
e invitations and polite requests: • *Will you come to dinner with me tonight?*
f the **first conditional** (see **Unit 18**): • *If you need me, I'll be there.*

Use **Shall I/Shall we** when offering help or suggestions.

The **present simple** is used for timetables, programmes and schedules:
- *The plane takes off at midnight.*   • *The president arrives at 3.30 p.m.*

A Complete the sentences with the most natural future form. More than one form may be possible.

1 Your car's still at the garage; it _____ ready by next Friday. (be)
2 What time _____ the overnight coach _____ from Manchester? (depart)
3 _____ we _____ our paintings up on the walls? Is that a good idea? (put)
4 She _____ at least £50 a month for next year's holiday. (save)
5 I'm afraid I can't come to your party; I _____ my grandmother in hospital. (visit)
6 _____ you _____ to my 21st birthday party? It's just for a few friends. (come)
7 I _____ never _____ anything as silly as that again, I promise! (do)
8 The phone's ringing. I _____ it. (answer)

B Match the two halves of the sentences. Use each item only once.

1 I don't think Joseph
2 The president and his party
3 She isn't going
4 There's someone at the door;
5 I'm sure
6 Shall we
7 Marion, will you
8 Surely you aren't
9 What time does the coach
10 I won't take any risks,

A to apply for that post.
B I'll never forget you.
C open the window for me, please?
D give you a hand with that?
E will get the job this time.
F depart on Sundays?
G going to give up now.
H so don't worry about me!
I you stay here, I'll see who it is.
J arrive in Washington at 9 p.m.

C Make questions and statements about the future, using the words in brackets.

1 What _____ this weekend? (you / do)

2 How long _____ ? (the journey from Milan to Brussels / take)

3 What _____ when you leave school? (you / do)

4 _____ with all that work? (I / help / you)

5 When _____ ? (the Stuttgart train / arrive)

6 _____ before we start the meeting? (I / shut the door)

7 Who _____ to the party on Saturday? (you / take)

8 Do you think _____ the match? (she / win)

9 _____ me? (you / marry)

10 _____ before we get the bill? (we / order some coffee)

11 Why _____ to the Canaries again this year? (you / not / go on holiday)

12 If there's enough time, _____ him to explain? (you / ask)

13 It's cold in here, isn't it? _____ the window. (I / close)

14 Don't worry! _____ you if you fall! (I / catch)

15 'Have you seen *Flash*?' 'No, but _____ it this evening.' (I / see)

D Here is your friend Jim's diary for next week. He's at university, studying Spanish and Economics. Imagine you are talking to Jim. Ask him questions about next week and work out his answers.

EXAMPLE:

What are you doing on Thursday afternoon?
I'm going to an Economics lecture.

MONDAY	Dentist 10 a.m.
	Spanish conversation class 11 a.m.
	Swim 12.30 p.m.
	Study for Economics exam at home (afternoon)
TUESDAY	Economics lecture (Room 12) 11 a.m.
	Meet Elaine for lunch at sandwich bar 12.30 p.m.
	Work in self-study centre 4–6 p.m.
	Go to Manuel's for supper 8 p.m.
WEDNESDAY	Spanish classes (Room 21) 9–11 a.m.
	Hair cut at Split Ends 12.00
	Keep-fit class 3 p.m.
	Meet Ali at Odeon cinema 7.30 p.m.
THURSDAY	Study in university library 9–12.00
	Economics lecture (Room 6) 2 p.m.
	Spanish lecture (Room 43) 4 p.m.
	Go to Darren's to study Economics with him 8 p.m.
FRIDAY	Economics EXAM! Lecture Hall 9–12.00
	Meet whole class for lunch at Roberto's Pizza House
	Football team practice 3–5 p.m.
	Meet Charles and Dora at Café Rouge 7.30 p.m.
SATURDAY	Do supermarket shopping (morning)
	Football match 2 p.m. (hope I play well!)
	Students' Disco 7 p.m.
SUNDAY	Get up late!
	Go for long walk with Elaine (morning)
	Lunch at Ali's house 1 p.m.
	Spanish homework (afternoon)
	Elaine, Manuel and Charles discuss holiday plans 8 p.m.

Recycling

A Complete the sentences, using the correct form of the verb in brackets.

1 Matt often _____ his guitar in the evening. (play)
2 What time _____ ? (you / usually / get up)
3 How many languages _____ ? (you / speak)
4 Sachiko always _____ her glasses for reading. (wear)
5 Ted _____ many photos when he goes on holiday. (not / take)
6 What _____ ? (this sentence / mean)
7 Philip _____ in an old house in the city centre. (live)
8 His mother still _____ in the bakery. (work)
9 My neighbour _____ to watch television most afternoons. (seem)
10 Those books _____ to you. (not belong)
11 Sandra _____ her hair three times a week. (wash)
12 _____ as well as he _____ he _____ ?
(your brother / cook, say, do)

B Match the two halves of the sentences. Use each item only once.

1 It's raining, so
2 The children are playing outside now,
3 Caroline is still ill,
4 He shouldn't drink anything,
5 Thanks, but I can't go out now
6 The boss is writing a report,
7 I see you're working on a project,
8 I'm really enjoying my holiday,
9 She's dancing down the street
10 We're watching television,

A but she's getting better.
B because I'm doing my homework.
C so I won't disturb you.
D but I don't like the hotel.
E I'm staying at home.
F because she's so happy!
G but there's nothing really worth watching.
H so don't bother him at the moment.
I but it will be dark soon.
J because he's driving.

C Some of these sentences are not correct. Tick (✔) the right ones, and correct the wrong ones.

1 I write a letter at the moment.
2 He's washing his car every Sunday afternoon.
3 She's living in a new flat now.
4 Are you talking to me or to him?
5 I'm flying to Munich on Sunday.
6 Look, the plane takes off.
7 He's Swiss and he's coming from Berne.
8 'Are you doing anything tonight?' 'I will borrow a video and watch it.'
9 Are you owning a house or a flat?
10 That looks heavy. Am I going to carry it for you?
11 I'm believing every word you say.
12 I promise I'm doing my best tomorrow.

D Match the questions and answers. Use each item only once.

1 Shall I tell you a story?
2 What's happening next door?
3 Can I help you, madam?
4 Why are you standing here?
5 What are you doing after supper?
6 What's your father doing at the moment?

A I'm just looking, thanks.
B I'm waiting for a bus.
C Go on, I'm listening.
D A baby's crying, I think.
E He's reading a newspaper.
F I'm going to a disco.

E Complete the second sentence so that it has a similar meaning to the first one. Use no more than **three** words.

1 There are fifteen jars in the cupboard.
The cupboard _____ fifteen jars.
2 My plan is to go to Australia very soon.
I'm _____ Australia very soon.
3 This problem is difficult to solve.
It is _____ to solve.
4 I'd like to invite you to lunch.
Will you _____ with me?
5 Liz doesn't very often go dancing.
Liz occasionally _____ dancing.
6 Can you explain this word to me, please?
What does _____ , please?
7 How long does the train journey from Pamplona to Madrid take?
When does the Pamplona train _____ Madrid?
8 You can trust me to finish the report on time.
I promise _____ the report on time.
9 I don't know where he lives.
Where _____ live?
10 That isn't my car.
That car _____ to me.

F Complete the sentences, using one of the following words:
don't isn't going do are doesn't was can't shall aren't

1 He _____ always give in his homework on time.
2 Oh dear, Lucy _____ going to win the match now.
3 How often _____ you wash your hair?
4 We haven't got any food, so I _____ cook the supper!
5 You haven't eaten your soup. _____ you like it?
6 Luckily the children _____ afraid of the dark.
7 There _____ hundreds of students in the lecture hall.
8 _____ I put the books away for you?
9 The party last night? Oh, yes, it _____ wonderful!
10 Dan's _____ to be an engineer when he finishes his training.

Possessives, demonstratives and reflexive pronouns

> **Possessive adjectives (my, his, her, our, your, their, its)** tell you who owns
> something: • *That's my pen!* • *Is this your coat?* • *We didn't take our car.*
>
> **Possessive pronouns (mine, his, hers, ours, yours, theirs)** are used instead of
> a possessive adjective plus a noun:
> • *My name's George. What's yours?* (= your name)
> • *That must be his* (= his car). *Ours* (= our car) is a Ford.

A Match the two halves of
the sentences. Use each
item only once.

1 I'm looking	A us his secret.
2 That must be mine –	B the boat is his or hers.
3 He didn't tell	C is it yours?
4 If ours doesn't start,	D their tickets at once.
5 It's my turn – or	E its facilities are excellent.
6 I don't know if	F all our information.
7 They wanted to book	G it's in my writing.
8 Don't give them	H shall we take theirs?
9 You can always	I for my gloves.
10 Try the York Hotel:	J rent her flat for a couple of days.

> **Demonstratives** are **this, that, these** and **those**. They are used to show
> or point to something or someone. **This** (singular) and **these** (plural) refer
> to things which are near, while **that** and **those** refer to things which are
> more distant:
> *A Is this your pen?* (holding it up)
> *B No, it isn't. That's mine.* (pointing to another one)
>
> You can use **this, that, these, those** in front of a noun, or alone if it is
> very clear what you mean: • *Is this the right train?* • *Do I have to pay
> for this?*
>
> There are also expressions with **this, that, these, those**:
> • *This is the life!* • *these days* • *Those were the days.* • *Is that all?*
> • *I don't like that kind of person.* • *This is Clare speaking.* • *Who's that?*
> • *How much is that altogether?* • *That's the right/wrong answer.*

B Some of these sentences
are not correct. Tick (✔) the
right ones, and correct the
wrong ones.

1 This people are always very kind and helpful.

2 That's the man, officer! I saw him robbing the post office!

3 I can't read any of these book – it's so boring.

4 All this cars are parked in the wrong place.

5 I liked that music very much.

6 How many of this exercises did you get right?

7 That are the students who were in my class.

8 Not many of those countries agreed to the plan.

9 Stop making all these noise at once!

10 Where did you get all those money from?

C Complete the sentences, using *this, that, these* or *those.*

1 Ah, wonderful! How relaxing! _____ is the life!

2 I'm afraid I don't like _____ kind of film.

3 Can you tell me where _____ apples over there come from?

4 Now, how much is _____ altogether, please?

5 I'm sorry, _____ isn't the right answer.

6 Which is your office, _____ one or that one?

7 Ah yes, _____ were the days, when we were young!

8 Families used to talk to each other more, but _____ days they just seem to watch television!

9 Only five people at the meeting? Is _____ all?

10 You know, _____ pasta is delicious. Try some!

Reflexive pronouns are used either when the subject and object are the same:
• *He cut himself while he was shaving.*   • *She told herself not to worry.*
or to stress the person who does something:
• *I made the dress myself.* (= I didn't buy it or ask anybody else to make it.)

D Complete the conversation with one of the following reflexive pronouns in each space:
herself himself myself ourselves yourself yourselves

Sandra: Jane and Wendy, come in. Do sit down. Help 1) _____ to some coffee and biscuits.

Wendy: Thanks. What a lovely room! Did you paint it 2) _____ ?

Sandra: Yes, most of it. My brother was helping me, but then he fell off the ladder and hurt 3) _____ , so I had to finish it 4) _____ .

Jane: Actually, Wendy and I decorated our flat 5) _____ . We think it looks great! And it was fun to do!

Sandra: My mother never does any work on her own house 6) _____ . She just pays someone to do it!

Wendy: Parents often think they know best!

E Complete the lists to check that you have understood this unit.

Subject	Object	Possessive adjective	Possessive pronoun	Reflexive pronoun
I	me	my	mine	myself
he	him	_____	_____	_____
she	her	_____	_____	_____
it	it	_____	_____	_____
we	us	_____	_____	_____
you	you	_____	_____	_____
they	them	_____	_____	_____

Past simple

The **past simple** is used to talk about completed actions at a particular point in the past, often with dates or times and words like **yesterday, last** and **ago**.

Regular verbs have an **-ed** or a **-d** ending:
• *Bill cycled to school yesterday, but Antonia walked all the way.*

There are many irregular verbs, which do not follow this pattern but have different endings (see page 128): • *She went to France in 2001.* • *We saw him last week.*

This is how you usually make the negative form, with **didn't**:
• *I'm sorry, I didn't hear what you said.* • *They didn't arrive on time.*

This is how you usually make a question, with **did**:
• *Did you buy anything in London?* • *How did he answer the question?*

Note that we do not use **did** in questions and negatives with the verb **be**:
• *Were you happy with the results?* • *She wasn't very interested in his story.*

A Complete the sentences, using one of the following verbs in the correct form. (Look them up on page 128 if you need to.)
bite buy cost drive forget make sleep take teach write

1 This jacket? Oh, I _____ it in one of those little boutiques.
2 I'm afraid I _____ too many photos on the trip.
3 I'm not going there again. Her dog _____ me, you know!
4 Shakespeare _____ *Hamlet* at the end of the sixteenth century.
5 The policeman _____ through the fog slowly and carefully.
6 Mike's father _____ him to play the trumpet.
7 'Was it very expensive?' 'Yes, it _____ a fortune!'
8 There was nowhere to stay, so I _____ in the back of the car.
9 'Did you turn off the lights?' 'Sorry, I _____ .'
10 I _____ a mistake, but luckily nobody noticed.

B Make these sentences positive or negative or questions, using the verbs given in capitals and the past simple.
EXAMPLES:
__ you __ the gas bill yesterday? PAY
***Did** you **pay** the gas bill yesterday?*
We flew to New York, but we __ to Dallas. FLY
*We flew to New York but we **didn't fly** to Dallas.*

1 Of course we _____ the house ourselves. We don't know anything about building! BUILD
2 _____ you _____ the key under the mat? LEAVE
3 I felt tired, so unfortunately I _____ to her party. GO
4 I'm very sorry I _____ the cup. Can I pay for a replacement? BREAK
5 The boys _____ their ball right into our garden. THROW
6 I _____ the money; I just borrowed it! STEAL
7 _____ your horse _____ the race yesterday? WIN
8 She _____ a cold at all last winter. CATCH
9 I had a map, so I _____ my way. LOSE
10 _____ the robbers _____ the jewels somewhere? HIDE
11 It's so sad! Nobody _____ me a birthday present! GIVE
12 You _____ much last week, did you? Only £10! SPEND

C Complete the story, using the following verbs in their correct form. (Look them up on page 128 if you need to.)

*arrive   be   break
cannot   come   fall
get up   have to   hear
hit   know   put   realise
return   say   think*

We 1)_____ all delighted when my Uncle Osmond 2)_____ all the way from Australia to visit us in England. But we soon 3)_____ that he was very accident-prone. On the first day he 4)_____ his arm while playing a game of cricket. We 5)_____ rush him to hospital, where the doctor in the emergency department 6)_____ his arm in plaster. A week later a golf ball 7)_____ Uncle Osmond on the head. At the hospital we were given a warm welcome by our doctor friend, who bandaged my uncle's head. Two days later Uncle Osmond 8)_____ a noise in the night and 9)_____ to investigate. He 10)_____ find the light switch, and 11)_____ downstairs. By now we 12)_____ the way to the hospital by heart, and we 13)_____ there in record time. The same doctor was on duty. 'Oh, it's you again!' he 14)_____ with a laugh. Uncle Osmond 15)_____ to Australia soon after this. He 16)_____ he would be safer at home!

D Now make questions the story, to fit these answers.

1 _____? Australia.
2 _____? His arm.
3 _____? On the head.
4 _____? Three times.
5 _____? Because he decided he would be safer there!

E Complete these past simple questions, using **one** word in each space.

1 _____ you paint that picture yourself?
2 _____ your brother still a teenager then?
3 _____ they pleased to see you, when you arrived?
4 _____ you promise to tell the truth at the time?
5 _____ you find any good bargains at the market?
6 _____ there any newspapers on the table yesterday morning?

Past continuous and past perfect

The **past continuous** is used to talk about an action in the past that went on for a long time.

Two continuous actions can happen at the same time:
• *He was listening to the radio while he was cooking.*
A short, completed action can interrupt a long, continuous one:
• *I was having a shower when suddenly I heard a scream.*

The **past continuous** can also be used to set the scene at the beginning of a story:
• *It was raining and the fog was getting thicker as we drove onto the motorway.*

Note the difference between the **past continuous** and the **past simple**:
• *What were you doing when the police arrived?* = What were you in the middle of doing ...?
• *What did you do when the police arrived?* = What was your next action ...?

A Complete the sentences, using one of the following verbs in the correct form:
do drive live talk wait walk wash watch

1 I _____ down the road when I saw the old lady fall over.
2 Paula _____ on her mobile phone all the time she was waiting in the queue.
3 When you rang last night, _____ she _____ her homework?
4 We _____ the 9 o'clock news on television when someone rang the door bell.
5 I bought this vase while I _____ with my family in Mexico City.
6 They _____ outside the cinema when we arrived.
7 I was amazed when I called to see Tony – he _____ the dishes while Anna was watching TV!
8 _____ you _____ the car when the accident happened?

B Use the past continuous to set the scene in these sentences, using the following verbs:
begin feel get shine sing

1 The sun _____ as we started our journey.
2 I _____ rather sad as I waved goodbye to my friends.
3 The birds _____ and it was a lovely day.
4 The rain _____ heavier, and there was more and more traffic.
5 It _____ to snow. It seemed a long way to walk.

C Choose the correct answer to each question from the alternatives in italics.

1 What were you doing when Caroline saw you in the café yesterday?
  I *was talking / talked* to my friends.
2 What were your friends doing when you arrived at the café?
  They *played / were playing* chess.
3 What did you all do when the fire alarm rang?
  We *ran / were running* into the street.
4 What did you do when you saw the flames?
  I *was helping / helped* to get other people out of the building.

> **The past perfect** is used to show that something happened **before** another past action (usually in the past simple):
> • *I'd* (= I had) *completely forgotten him until I saw him again last week.*
> • *She booked a holiday in Florida, because she'd* (= she had) *heard so much about it.*

D Complete the sentences, using the past perfect of the verb in brackets. Which is the first action in each sentence?

1 She was delighted. She _____ all her exams! (pass)

2 I recognised the village because I _____ there before. (be)

3 We didn't go to the cinema because we _____ that film. (already / see)

4 He _____ alone until he went to university. (never / live)

5 The manager was angry with Kate because she _____ the letters. (not / send)

6 I _____ her until you introduced me at the party. (not / meet)

7 When the reporters arrived, the firemen _____ the fire. (already / put out)

8 I was very nervous about my new job, because I _____ in a call centre before. (never / work)

E Match the two halves of the sentences. Which is the first action in each sentence?

1 We stayed at the White Rocks Hotel

2 I'd just posted the letter

3 My sister had never eaten snails

4 By the time I got to the party,

5 When the mechanic arrived,

A when I realised I'd forgotten to put a stamp on it.

B nearly all the guests had left.

C I'd already managed to start the car.

D because a friend had recommended it.

E until she went to Strasbourg last year.

F Correct the sentences if necessary. Tick (✔) any which are already correct. Be careful – some of them don't need the past perfect!

1 We finished our lunch and had left the restaurant soon afterwards.

2 When Clive passed his driving test, his father had bought him a car.

3 I had no idea where your friends lived.

4 Stuart offered his credit card, but I'd already paid the bill.

5 The concert was sold out because there had been a lot of advance publicity.

Present perfect simple and continuous

The **present perfect** is used to talk about recent actions at no fixed time, often with **just, already, recently, lately**:
- *The Democrats have won the election.*   • *We've just seen elephants in the park!*
and also actions with a result or effect in the present:
- *Oh no, I've lost my purse!*   • *Her car's broken down.*
and actions or experiences which are not finished, often with **yet, so far, ever**:
- *'Have you ever been to Denmark?' 'No, I haven't been there yet.'*

For with the present perfect covers a period of time, but **since** with the present perfect refers to a fixed point of time in the past:
- *We've lived here for five years.*   • *I haven't seen you since my birthday.*

A Use the words given to make present perfect sentences. Remember to check irregular verb forms on page 128.

1 I / not / write / to him often enough.
2 Penny / switch off / the television yet?
3 They / nearly / finish / their work, and it's only lunchtime!
4 He / save / a lot of money since January.
5 You / ever / see / a flying fish?
6 You / see / any good films lately?
7 We really / not / make / much progress so far.
8 You can relax. I / already / do / the shopping.

B Complete the sentences with *for* or *since*.

1 She's been waiting _____ half an hour.
2 They haven't seen each other _____ 1989.
3 _____ last week the prices have gone up.
4 I'm hoping to stay here _____ six months.
5 The professor has already been talking _____ an hour.
6 They've been dancing _____ eight o'clock.
7 I've worked for that company _____ four years now.
8 The manager has taken on three more assistants _____ last summer.

C Put the words in the right order, to make correct sentences.

1 haven't Fred we a time seen for long
2 office she the has to gone post
3 her not Susan moved flat has into new yet
4 cat just my had has kittens
5 already I've bill paid the
6 garden he a tree new his in has planted fruit
7 started engineers now the work have
8 only holiday she her just has back come from

D Some of these sentences are not correct. Tick (✔) the right ones, and correct the wrong ones.

1 I have bought the car last year.

2 Jane hasn't done her homework yet.

3 Have you ever been to Paris?

4 I am here since January 1st.

5 They never eaten fish and chips before.

6 He's just passed his driving test.

7 My friends are already studying English for ten years.

8 That was a great film we've seen last night.

The **present perfect continuous** shows that actions which started in the past are still happening, or have only recently stopped but have a result or effect in the present:
- *I've been waiting here for ages.* (= I'm still here.)
- *You look very tired. Have you been working too hard?*

E Complete the sentences, using the present perfect continuous of the verb in brackets and either *for* (a period of time) or *since* (a fixed point of time).

1 She _____ (study) German _____ she arrived in Berlin.

2 They _____ (wait) outside _____ a very long time.

3 I _____ (save up) to buy a motorbike _____ last year.

4 You _____ (type) letters _____ at least two hours.

5 He _____ (go) to evening classes _____ six weeks.

6 You _____ (work) hard _____ I last saw you.

7 _____ the last ten years they _____ (live) in India.

8 Ever_____ he met Amy, he _____ (learn) Chinese.

F Complete the sentences by deciding whether to use the present perfect (continuous) or the past simple of the verb in brackets. Look at the study boxes in this unit and **Unit 7** before you start.

1 Yesterday the local team _____ their match. (win)

2 I'm sorry, I _____ what you said. (not / hear)

3 Hello! What _____ recently? (you / do)

4 _____ any presents for your family yet? (you / buy)

5 I _____ to play the piano when I was very young. (learn)

6 Sorry, I _____ to lock the door when I left the house. (forget)

7 _____ to Abu Dhabi? (you / ever / be)

8 _____ interested in the job they gave to John? (you / be)

9 How long _____ Japanese up to now? (you / study)

10 I think she _____ her driving test. (just / pass)

11 They _____ that house ten years ago. (buy)

12 Oh dear! I think I _____ my pen! (lose)

13 We _____ to this area in 2000. (move)

14 _____ well last night? (you / sleep)

15 The students _____ excellent progress so far. (make)

Recycling

A Complete this story, using the verbs in brackets in their correct form.

Last week I 1) _____ (be) at my desk in the classroom as usual. I 2) _____ (feel) rather tired, and 3) _____ (can / not) concentrate on the lesson. I 4) _____ (look) round and 5) _____ (notice) a door behind me. 'I'm sure it 6) _____ (be / not) there before!' I 7) _____ (say) to myself. Very quietly I 8) _____ (get up), 9) _____ (open) the door, and 10) _____ (see) a long, dark corridor ahead of me. I 11) _____ (start) walking down the corridor. Soon I 12) _____ (find) myself in an underground room. There 13) _____ (be) a lot of unpleasant-looking machines, and people 14) _____ (move) around in white coats. Suddenly I 15) _____ (hear) a scream from another room, and 16) _____ (begin) to feel frightened. Just then a tall, cruel-looking man with white hair 17) _____ (come) towards me.

'I am the Professor,' he 18) _____ (tell) me. 'How nice to see you! 19) _____ (you / come) to help with our little experiment?' I 20) _____ (not / like) the Professor, and I 21) _____ (not / want) to stay. I 22) _____ (try) to run away, but my legs 23) _____ (not / move). He 24) _____ (come) closer. 'Don't worry,' he 25) _____ (say), smiling. 'We're just doing a few tests ...' 'No!' I 26) _____ (shout). 'No tests!' He 27) _____ (put) his hand on my arm and 28) _____ (repeat), 'A few tests, tests, tests ...'

Just then I 29) _____ (wake up). I 30) _____ (be) back in the classroom, and someone 31) _____ (shake) my arm. I listened to the teacher. 'Tests this week and next week,' she 32) _____ (say). 'That's better,' I 33) _____ (think).

B Match the two halves of the sentences. Use each item only once.

1 My mother always laughs	A	flows through Stratford.
2 The River Avon	B	buy a bike?
3 Jamie often forgets	C	understand Russian at all.
4 Why don't you	D	eating cheese or strawberries.
5 Ella's parents	E	at my father's jokes.
6 Roger doesn't	F	people's names.
7 The students come	G	both live in Bonn.
8 Hilary doesn't like	H	all kinds of fish.
9 Cats eat	I	hope to stay here?
10 How long do you	J	from Slovakia.

C Read the text and choose the correct word or phrase (A, B, C, or D) for each space.

It all started when Edward had to travel to an important meeting in Birmingham by train. The sun was 1) _____ when he got on the train, and he felt sleepy because he 2) _____ gone to bed late the night before. So he fell asleep as soon as the train 3) _____ . He woke up suddenly when the train stopped at a station, and 4) _____ another passenger, wearing a business suit, getting off the train *with Edward's briefcase!* 'Hey!' Edward 5) _____ . 'Come back! That's 6) _____ !' The station master heard Edward, and 7) _____ to

the businessman, 'Excuse me, sir, is that 8) _____ ?' The man looked
very angry. Just then Edward realised that 9) _____ briefcase was
beside him on the seat; he 10) _____ noticed it at first. 'It's OK,' he
called, '11) _____ found my case. I'm so sorry, I 12) _____ a
mistake.' Edward told 13) _____ to be more careful in future, and
never 14) _____ to sleep on a train again.

	A	B	C	D
1	shone	shining	shine	shines
2	has	is	had	have
3	started	starts	starting	start
4	sees	seen	seeing	saw
5	shouted	shouts	shout	shouting
6	my	me	mine	my one
7	says	said	saying	say
8	yours	you	your	your one
9	him	whose	he's	his
10	had	hadn't	hasn't	didn't
11	I'd	I'm	I've	I'll
12	made	making	make	makes
13	him	himself	he	herself
14	goes	gone	went	going

D Complete the second sentence so that it has a similar meaning to the first one. Use no more than **three** words.

1 I haven't been to Portugal since 2001.
   I last _____ in 2001.

2 When did you start your course?
   How long have _____ your course?

3 She didn't get anyone to repair the car for her.
   She _____ herself.

4 We went to Chicago for the first time.
   We had _____ to Chicago before.

5 I know it belongs to them, because there's a label on it.
   I know it's _____ , because there's a label on it.

6 I recognised him at once.
   I knew at once I _____ before.

7 The police arrived too late, so the robber escaped.
   By the time the police arrived, _____ escaped.

8 Do you know Argentina at all?
   Have you ever _____ to Argentina?

9 When did you buy your computer?
   How long have _____ your computer?

10 The phone call interrupted my breakfast.
   I was _____ when the phone rang.

Definite and indefinite articles

> We use the indefinite article **an** in front of words beginning with **a, e, i, o, u** – and **h** when it is not sounded: • *an umbrella, an hour.* We use **a** in front of all other letters, and in front of **u** and **eu** when they sound like 'you': • *a university, a European.*
>
> **A/an** is used for singular countable nouns: • *Have a cup of tea.*
> It is used for jobs: • *She's a teacher.*
> and for certain numbers, quantities and costs:
> • *a hundred*   • *20 kilometres an hour*   • *£200 a kilo*   • *twenty times a day*
>
> The definite article **the** is used for a person or thing already mentioned or known, after *play* with musical instruments, and for some important buildings, names of rivers, seas, mountain ranges and groups of islands or states:
> • *play the drums*   • *the Town Hall*   • *the Atlantic*   • *the Andes*
> and also when there is only one of something: • *the sun*   • *the kitchen*
>
> **The** is not used for most street names (except *the High Street*), most countries, lakes, after *play* with sports, or for expressions like *at/to work, at/go home, at/to school,* or for generalising: • *I like black coffee.*   • *Life is difficult for him.*   • *Time flies.*

A Complete the phrases and sentences with *a, an, the* or – .

1 He's ____ engineer.
2 She plays ____ guitar.
3 We stayed at ____ home.
4 ____ brown bread is better than white.
5 She lives near ____ Lake Geneva.
6 Ricardo's? It's ____ Italian restaurant.
7 He's ____ honest man.
8 We visited ____ Philippines.
9 Go down ____ High Street.
10 The plums are 80 pence ____ kilo.
11 They went climbing in ____ Alps.
12 It's ____ United Nations plan.

B Complete the sentences, using one of the following nouns or names. Use *a, an, the* or – where necessary.
cinema   France
moment   music
North Street   office
phone   problem   tennis
time

1 Last night we wanted to see a film, so we went to _____ .
2 He'll be here soon; just wait _____ .
3 I'm sorry I haven't written lately. I just haven't had _____ .
4 Last summer they spent their holiday in _____ .
5 The new house is near a sports centre, so we can swim and play _____ .
6 If you come round to my place this evening, we can do our keep-fit exercises together and listen to _____ .
7 Simon's trying to finish a report, so he's still at _____ .
8 Don't worry about it; I promise it won't be _____ .
9 I need to ring someone. Do you mind if I use _____ ?
10 Sorry, which road do you live in? In _____ ?

Modal verbs

Modal verbs tell us the speaker's mood or opinion.

Must is used to show what is necessary: • *You must renew your passport.*
and what is probably true: • *Hasn't she come to school? She must be ill.*

Mustn't shows what is forbidden or not allowed:
• *You mustn't talk during the exam.*

Can is used when asking for something, or to show what people are able to do:
• *Can I have the salt, please?*   • *She can speak five languages.*
or when offering to help: • *I can do your shopping for you.*

May/Might show that something is possible in the future:
• *It may rain tonight.*   • *She might pass the exam, but I don't think so.*
and are used when asking for something: • *May I leave now?*

Ought to/Should show what the speaker thinks is the correct thing to do or say:
• *You should tell him at once.*   • *He ought to be more polite.*

Note that **do/did** are not used in questions or negatives with these verbs.

A Match the statements or questions with the responses. Use each item only once.

1 You really must work harder.
2 It's strange, Liz isn't here yet.
3 I can help, if you like.
4 May I borrow your iron?
5 I wonder if he'll get the job.
6 You mustn't go in there!
7 Can we bring the dog?
8 She ought to stay in bed.
9 Can you drive?
10 I think we should stop now.

A Yes, that's what the doctor suggests.
B He might, but I don't think so.
C Oh, all right, but keep him on a lead.
D I promise I will.
E That's kind of you.
F Why not? What's inside?
G Of course – here it is.
H Yes, we've done enough.
I She must be on her way.
J Yes, I've had a licence since I was eighteen.

B Complete the sentences, using one of the following modal verbs:
can   may   mustn't   should   ought

1 You _____ park right outside the hospital entrance. You'll be in the way.
2 He's very busy at the moment, but he _____ come to the party.
3 You really _____ stop worrying about your brother.
4 Excuse me, but you _____ to be more careful with that knife.
5 _____ I have the results as soon as possible, please?

Question words and relative pronouns

Question words can be used to introduce a question.

Who asks about a person: • *Who are you?*

Why asks for a reason: • *Why did you do that?*

Where asks about a place: • *Where are you going?*

What asks for information: • *What is your name?*

How asks about ways of doing things:
• *A How did you learn English? B By studying hard!*
But note: • *A How are you? How's the family? How's life? B Fine, thanks.*

How long asks about length of time: • *How long are you staying here?*

How many asks about numbers: • *How many plates do you need?*

How much asks about quantity, often money: • *How much does it cost?*

When asks about times of things that have happened or may happen:
• *When were you born?*   • *When are you coming to visit us?*

Whose asks who owns something: • *Whose is this book?*

Which asks about choosing between two or more things: • *Which do you prefer?*

How often asks about the frequency of actions:
• *A How often do you go shopping? B Once a month / Twice a week / Every day.*

A Imagine you have just met someone new at a friend's house. Complete the questions that you might ask him or her.

Then write down any other questions you can think of, starting with a question word.

1 _____ do you live?

2 _____ have you been living there?

3 _____ is your name? _____ does everybody call you?

4 _____ are you studying? Do you like it there?

5 _____ are you going to do when you leave school / university?

6 _____ kind of music do you like?

7 _____ is your favourite singer or group?

8 _____ are your hobbies? _____ do you spend your free time?

9 _____ countries have you visited?

10 _____ is your phone number?!

B Look at the situations and ask a suitable question in each case.

1 You've found a watch on the floor in the classroom. You want to give it back to the owner, but you don't know who that is.

2 You've met a girl who isn't English but speaks the language well. You think she must have studied English for a long time. Ask her.

3 Your teacher has corrected your homework exercise, but you can't understand your mistakes. Ask why the exercise is wrong.

4 Your friends all went to the disco last weekend, but you were ill and couldn't go. Now you want to know the names of the people who were there.

5 You are babysitting for your aunt, who leaves you in her house to look after her children. You aren't sure how to switch on the heating/ air conditioning. Ask her.

6 You really like your friend's schoolbag, and want to buy one exactly like it. You need to know the price.

7 You are surprised to find that your friend has already done his homework. You want to know when he did it.

8 You'd like to know where your parents are planning to go on holiday next year.

9 Someone has just run into the room, picked up your dictionary and rushed out. You want to know why they did that.

10 You want to know the name of a book your friend is reading.

Who, which, that, what, why, where, when and **whose** are called **relative pronouns** when they connect parts of sentences.

Who refers to a person: • *She's the one who took the money.*

Which and **that** refer to a thing: • *the hotel which/that we recommended*

What means 'the thing that': • *I told him what he should do.*

Why refers to a reason, **where** to a place, **when** to a time, and **whose** to something belonging to someone:
• *That's the reason why we did it.*   • *Is that where the accident happened?*
• *It's the time of year when tourists start coming.*
• *It's the man whose house was on fire.*

C Match the two halves of the sentences and connect them with *who, which, whose, why* or *where*. Use each item only once.

1 We visited the town
2 Can you tell me
3 That's the child
4 I talked to the doctor,
5 They stayed in a five-star hotel,

A toy is missing.
B advised me to wait.
C Shakespeare was born.
D was very expensive.
E you don't like vegetables?

D Complete the text with relative pronouns from the second study box.

The two old ladies 1) _____ lived next door were called Joanna and Martha. They were sisters, and had lived there all their lives. Martha was the quiet one, 2) _____ stayed at home and did the housework. She always wore a white apron, 3) _____ never looked dirty. Joanna, 4) _____ was more sociable, was a secretary until she reached sixty and retired. 'I've had enough of that office,' she told Martha. But that wasn't the real reason 5) _____ she stopped working. She had always dreamed of going on a long, expensive holiday, to beautiful cities, 6) _____ she could spend days in art galleries and museums, and to white sandy beaches, 7) _____ she could sunbathe and swim.
And now she had the time and the money to do 8) _____ she wanted. But she knew that Martha, 9) _____ was so different from her, and 10) _____ only interest was the house, would not like the idea.

Countables and uncountables

Some is used for people or things, and when offering something:
- *She's got some very nice friends.*   • *Would you like some honey?*

Any is used in a question or negative:
- *Is there any water in the bottle?*   • *I haven't taken any photos yet.*

English nouns are either **countable** (like *table, student, child, potato*) or **uncountable** (like *money, water, bread, butter, news, information*).

A Decide whether the following words are countable (C) or uncountable (U).

progress	____	vegetables	____	advice	____
bread	____	meat	____	news	____
air	____	water	____	wine	____
money	____	knowledge	____	shoe	____
tomato	____	tea	____	sugar	____
information	____	people	____	book	____
sand	____	gold	____	car	____
student	____	rooms	____	furniture	____

Some, a lot of, a few are used with countable nouns in the plural.
Some, a lot of, a little are used with uncountable nouns.

Any and **many** are used for plural countables in a question or negative.
Any and **much** are used for uncountables in a question or negative.

B Underline the correct alternative.

1 only *a little* / *a few* information
2 not *much* / *many* wine
3 only *a little* / *a few* tomatoes
4 not *much* / *many* bread

5 not *much* / *many* people
6 only *a few* / *a little* money
7 not *much* / *many* cars
8 only *a few* / *a little* advice

C Match the two halves of the sentences. Use each item only once.

1 How much
2 He's got a lot of
3 There were only a few
4 Would you like some
5 She hasn't bought any
6 She didn't give us much
7 I'd just like a little
8 Do you know how many
9 We'll take some
10 Has she made any

A people in the audience last night.
B make-up this month.
C money can you lend me?
D news in her letter.
E sugar in my tea, please.
F books you will have to buy?
G coffee now?
H sandwiches with us.
I progress this term?
J information on his computer.

Recycling

A Complete the story, putting **one** word in each space.

Linda Evans was 1) _____ well-known writer of children's stories, 2) _____ lived in a charming old cottage in Devon. Normally she worked at 3) _____ , in her quiet, peaceful study. Long 4) _____ her books became popular, she 5) _____ managed to teach 6) _____ how to use a computer, and now typed all her stories on her PC. But sometimes she had to leave her cottage to get 7) _____ information from the library or have a meeting with 8) _____ publisher. She hated being away, because she was very worried about burglars. So she always locked the house up extremely 9) _____ . Just before leaving, she always put 10) _____ full cup of coffee on the kitchen table, and left the radio playing, to make a burglar think 11) _____ was someone at home.

One day she came 12) _____ after a day out, and 13) _____ at once that someone 14) _____ been there. There was only a 15) _____ coffee left in the cup, and the radio was off. But when she looked at her computer, she saw it was switched on, and someone had typed in a new story. She had no idea 16) _____ had got in, or how, because none of the doors or windows were damaged. But she sat down to read the story, and it was a very good one. 'I'll use it in my next book!' she 17) _____ happily.

The next month she had to go to London for the day. She 18) _____ a pot of coffee and a plate of sandwiches on the table. When she returned, the coffee and sandwiches 19) _____ gone. She ran to the computer. This time there was only a message on the screen. 'IT'S NOT *YOUR* STORY, IT'S 20) _____ !' it said.

B Underline the correct alternative in the sentences.

1 There isn't *any / some* tea left in the pot.
2 Susie has *much / a lot of* cassettes in her room.
3 Would you like *some / much* cream with your fruit?
4 Wasn't there *a few / any* paper in the printer?
5 He asked his lawyer for *a little / a few* advice.
6 Only *a little / a few* people respect the rules.
7 Thomas hasn't got *many / much* work to do today.
8 I'd better get *a few / some* money from the bank.
9 There aren't *many / a few* flowers in the garden.
10 Is there *some / any* news from your family?
11 Could you give me *many / some* information, please?
12 We didn't like *any / a few* of the music.
13 *Some / A little* students always get good marks.
14 You can have *much / a few* more sandwiches if you like.
15 We haven't got *some / much* idea of how many guests are coming to the party.

C Complete the sentences using one of the following words or phrases in each space. Use **the** where necessary.

big dogs   Bulgaria   flute
green tea   home
ice hockey   literature
love   raw fish   Town Hall

1 Meet me at _____ . We can get some tourist information there.
2 _____ is worth studying in any language.
3 Rodrigo plays _____ in his school orchestra.
4 We had to go _____ before the meeting, to collect our files.
5 Have you ever tried _____ ? The Chinese often drink it with their meals.
6 My favourite sport is _____ .
7 *Only You*, a beautifully romantic song about _____ , is at number 1 in the pop charts.
8 I think he comes from _____ . What language does he speak?
9 _____ is very popular in some countries, but it must be eaten very fresh.
10 Matthew is afraid of _____ , because he was attacked by one once.

D Complete the second sentence so that it has a similar meaning to the first one. Use no more than **three** words.

1 It would be a good idea for you to see a doctor.
I think you _____ a doctor.
2 I'm afraid you are not allowed to smoke here.
Sorry, but you _____ here.
3 I think he's able to speak French very well.
I think he _____ French very well.
4 Did you see that girl? Her brother won an Olympic medal.
That's the girl _____ an Olympic medal.
5 When are you going to leave?
How long are _____ stay?
6 It won't be possible for me to come tomorrow.
I'm afraid I _____ tomorrow.
7 Excuse me, could you explain this word?
Excuse me, what _____ mean?
8 It's very important to keep your passport in a safe place.
You really _____ your passport in a safe place.
9 Laura left England for the last time in 1999.
Laura hasn't been to England _____ 1999.
10 Sorry, is it OK if I borrow your guidebook?
Excuse me, _____ borrow your guidebook?
11 I saw him take the money – he's the thief!
He's the thief – he _____ the money!
12 Halfway through dinner there was a knock on the door.
There was a knock on the door while we _____ dinner.

UNIT 16

Passives

> The **passive** is used when an action or state is more important than the person who does it:
> - *The palace was built in the eighteenth century.*   • *He was called Honest Joe.*
> - *A thousand cars were produced last week.*   • *I was born in Coventry.*
> or when we do not know who did it:
> - *The bank was robbed on Monday.* (The police may not know who the robbers are.)
>
> The **passive** is formed with the subject of the sentence, plus the verb **be** in the correct tense, and the past participle of the verb you want:
> - *The photos were taken quickly.*   • *The house will be painted tomorrow.*
>
> Sometimes we add **by** plus the person or thing doing the action, but only if we feel the information is really necessary, and not if it is just a pronoun (like *you, me*):
> - *The diamonds were found by Lady Caroline's private detective.*

A Use the words given to make sentences in the passive. Check the list of irregular verbs on page 128.

1 Biscuits / make / that factory
2 The secret agent / arrest / Zurich airport last week
3 The key / keep / that box
4 Hazel / teach / Miss Jones last year, I think
5 The grass / always cut / every week
6 you / give / the right information yesterday?
7 You / not invite / to the party a fortnight ago
8 the stolen car / ever / find?

B Complete the passive sentences, using the correct form of the following verbs:
check   eat   export   give
hurt   lock   see   speak

1 John _____ a mobile phone for his birthday.
2 Those doors _____ yesterday. They were left open.
3 All the food _____ at Jaime's party yesterday.
4 English _____ in this restaurant.
5 Passports _____ usually _____ at the airport.
6 The escaped prisoner _____ in Liverpool – someone even took a photo of him.
7 Coffee _____ in huge quantities by Brazil.
8 My friend _____ badly _____ in the accident, but now he's made a complete recovery.

C Match the two halves of the sentences. Use each item only once.

1 Our car is always serviced
2 The fruit was picked
3 I was born
4 Were you planning
5 Alexander was called
6 That cake was made

A twenty-five years ago.
B Alex by most of his friends.
C to join the club?
D with six eggs.
E in Spain and then frozen.
F at the local garage.

Prepositions

At, in, on, to are prepositions of place.

At is used for an address with a number, or a building:
- *He lives at 7 Dyke Road.*   • *I'll see you at the cinema.*   • *I'm at home today.*

In is used for a street, town, region, country or continent: • *They work in Malaysia.*
or an enclosed space: • *The money is in his briefcase.*

On usually refers to a flat surface:
- *The picture is on the wall.*   • *There are books on the shelf.*

To is used with verbs of movement: • *They flew from Sydney to Hong Kong.*

Note that *arrive* is never followed by **to** but only by **at** or **in**:
- *She arrived at Larnaca Airport.*   • *He arrived in Germany yesterday.*

Remember that we usually say someone has been **to** a place (a short visit), not **in**:
- *He's been to Prague recently.*

Note that we say **at the top / bottom, on the left / right, in the centre / middle**, when describing a picture or map.

A Complete the sentences with the correct preposition.

1 I'm just going ____ the bank.
2 We'll meet you ____ the Theatre Royal.
3 There is some food ____ the table.
4 The museum is ____ Western Road.
5 I've never been ____ Poland.
6 We arrived ____ Portugal today.
7 I live ____ 21 New Road.

8 Do your parents live ____ Rome?
9 She's driving ____ Helsinki tomorrow.
10 She's studying ____ Hove College.
11 He's staying ____ the Ritz Hotel.
12 His clothes are ____ the floor.
13 He went ____ Athens last weekend.
14 The milk is ____ the fridge.

Other common prepositions of place are **near, in front of, opposite, behind, next to, under**:
- *Glen's house is near the church.* • *The post office is next to Glen's house.*
- *Behind the church you can see the hills.* • *The park is opposite the church / Glen's house.* • *Glen is standing in front of the post office.*
- *Ducks are swimming under the bridge.*

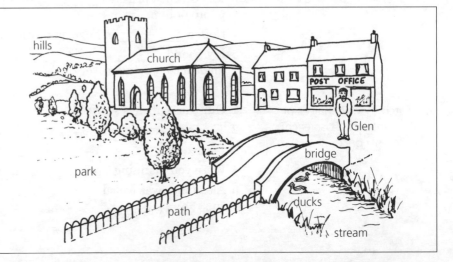

B Look at the picture of Glen's bedroom, and complete the sentences with the correct preposition.

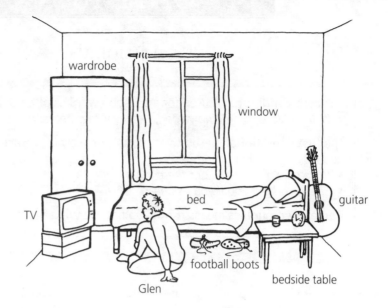

1 His football boots are _____ the bed.

2 The wardrobe is _____ the window.

3 _____ the bed you can see a guitar.

4 _____ the bed is a bedside table.

5 Glen is sitting _____ the television.

6 The bed is _____ the window.

At, in, on are also used to talk about time.

At is used for exact times, festivals and mealtimes:
• *at 3 o'clock, at Easter, at the weekend, at breakfast time, at night*
Note that *at night* is much more common than *in the night*, but we say *in the middle of the night*.

In is used for seasons, years, months and times of day:
• *in spring, in 1952, in April, in the morning*

On is used for days of the week, dates and special days:
• *on Monday, on 17th May, on Christmas Day*

Note that we write *24th March*, but we say *It's the 24th of March*.

C Complete the phrases with the correct preposition.

1 ____ Easter Day	8 ____ autumn	15 ____ 4.15 p.m.
2 ____ 1886	9 ____ 1st August	16 ____ the evening
3 ____ the weekend	10 ____ September	17 ____ Christmas
4 ____ night	11 ____ lunchtime	18 ____ Thursday
5 ____ 27th March 1992	12 ____ May 14th	19 ____ midnight
6 ____ Monday morning	13 ____ summer	20 ____ the afternoon
7 ____ St Valentine's Day	14 ____ your birthday	21 ____ eight o'clock

Conditionals

> The **zero conditional** is used for a situation which is often or always true:
> • *If Henry does something wrong, he never says he's sorry.*
>
> The **first conditional** is used for a possible or likely future action which depends on another action:
> • *If we take a taxi, we'll get there in time.*
> • *She'll work for you if you ask her.*
>
> **Remember** – **unless** means **if not**. Do not use **will** after **if**.

A Match the two halves of the zero conditional sentences, and connect them with *if* or *unless*. Use each item only once.

1 Most houseplants die
2 People get extremely angry
3 Water freezes
4 You can't see the doctor
5 We often go camping
6 You can ask a policeman
7 We can ski in the Sierra Nevada
8 Jerry only helps people
9 I usually have a big birthday party
10 You can't go all that way by car

A it is below 0° Celsius.
B I am short of money!
C there is enough snow.
D you don't give them water.
E you need tourist information.
F you have two drivers.
G he knows and likes them.
H buses are late in the rush hour.
I the weather is fine at weekends.
J you make an appointment.

B Complete the first conditional sentences with your own endings for 1–6, and your own ideas for beginnings for 7–12.

1 If I can't do my homework this afternoon, _____ .

2 If there's nothing good on TV tonight, _____ .

3 If Sonia invites me to her party this weekend, _____ .

4 If we miss the bus home after school, _____ .

5 If my parents ask me where we should go on holiday, _____ .

6 If I pass all my exams brilliantly, _____ .

7 _____ , I'll be delighted.

8 _____ , I'll suggest a mountain bike, or a DVD player.

9 _____ , I'll accept at once.

10 _____ , I'll work much harder next year.

11 _____ , I'll eat less and take lots of exercise.

12 _____ , I'll refuse, politely, of course!

> The **second conditional** is used for a possible, not probable, future situation:
> * *If I won the lottery, I'd travel round the world.*
>
> It can also be used for an imaginary situation, the opposite of the real present situation:
> * *If I had more money, I'd buy a new car.* (I have an old car and not much money.) and also for giving advice:
> * *If I were you, I'd buy it at once.*

C Complete the second conditional sentences with the correct form of the verbs in brackets.

1 If you _____ (tell) me the truth, I _____ (believe) you.
2 I _____ (can) collect you from the station if you _____ (let) me know the time of your train.
3 If I _____ (be) you, I _____ (buy) some new clothes for the party.
4 If you _____ (go) by plane, you _____ (get) there much faster.
5 But if you _____ (go) by coach, it _____ (cost) much less.

D What would you do in these situations? Answer the questions with *I'd* ...

What would you do if ...
1 ... you saw a house on fire?
2 ... you saw someone lying unconscious on the pavement?
3 ... a beggar asked you for money in the street?
4 ... you got on a train without a ticket?
5 ... you found you had no money when you arrived at the supermarket checkout with all your shopping?

E Complete the second sentence so that it has a similar meaning to the first one. Use no more than **three** words.

1 I'm too hungry to concentrate properly.
  If I weren't so hungry, _____ able to concentrate properly.
2 Perhaps I could go to Spain and visit José.
  If I went to Spain, _____ José.
3 I don't speak Arabic well enough to work in Egypt.
  If I _____ better, I could work in Egypt.
4 I think you should stop smoking.
  If I _____ , I'd stop smoking.
5 My dream is to become rich and successful, and buy a castle.
  If I _____ and successful, I'd buy a castle.

F Give a friend of yours some advice in these situations, starting with *If I were you* ... each time.

1 He's got a bad headache.
2 She's lost her credit card somewhere.
3 He's in love with the girl next door.
4 She watches too much television.
5 He's just crashed his father's car.
6 She hasn't done any work for her exams.
7 He's a bit overweight.
8 She wants to spend £300 on a coat.

UNIT 19

Comparatives and superlatives

When we compare two people or things, we use **more** or **less** for long adjectives, and **-er** for short ones, with **than**:
- *Sofia is more intelligent than Josef.*   • *Paolo is taller than his brother.*

Sometimes we use **(not) as ... as**:
- *She wasn't as kind as Fatima.*   • *He's just as charming as his brother.*

Note these exceptions:
- *good ~ better*   • *bad ~ worse*   • *far ~ further / farther*

and be careful with spelling:
- *happy ~ happier*   • *fat ~ fatter*

A Write down the correct comparatives for these adjectives.

1 difficult	6 happy	11 dark	16 red
2 clever	7 far	12 convenient	17 modern
3 comfortable	8 big	13 beautiful	18 ugly
4 easy	9 bad	14 intelligent	19 delicious
5 good	10 helpful	15 untidy	20 sunny

B Compare these pairs of people or things, using *not as ... as*.

Then make eight sentences, using *more* or *less* or *-er* and *than*. Make sure your sentences make good sense!

Example:
1 *Your room is untidier than mine.*

1 My room	untidy	yours.
2 Your teacher	helpful	mine.
3 Living in a village	much fun	living in a town.
4 Biscuits	good for your health	fresh fruit.
5 A bike	convenient in the rain	a car.
6 English	difficult to learn	Chinese.
7 A cake	easy to cook	an omelette.
8 Josie	good at meeting people	Giorgio.

C Complete the conversation, using comparatives.

A So which camera are you going to buy, then?

B I'm not sure. This one's 1) _____ expensive, but it's got a better name 2) _____ the other one. What do you think?

A I'd go for the 3) _____ one – you don't want to spend too much money on it. It's 4) _____ , as well – the other one's very heavy.

B But will the expensive one take 5) _____ pictures? I really want good quality photos.

A Don't worry about that. Cameras all take good pictures these days.

B OK. If it's just as good 6) _____ the other, I'll take the cheaper, lighter one that nobody's ever heard of!

The **superlative** is used when we talk about the best, the worst, the most attractive people or the most useful things in the class, in the room, in the world. We use **the most** or **the least** for long adjectives, and **the + -est** for shorter adjectives:
- *the most popular film*   • *the longest river in the world*   • *the prettiest picture*

Note these exceptions:
- *good ~ the best*   • *bad ~ the worst*   • *far ~ the furthest / farthest*
and be careful with spelling:
- *ugly ~ the ugliest*   • *thin ~ the thinnest*   • *wide ~ the widest*

D Write down the correct superlatives for these adjectives.

1 good	6 rich	11 far	16 tidy
2 fat	7 useful	12 comfortable	17 strong
3 happy	8 bad	13 wide	18 pretty
4 young	9 ugly	14 thin	19 white
5 difficult	10 long	15 romantic	20 fast

E Complete the sentences with the correct superlative.

1 At 8848 metres Mount Everest in the Himalayas is _____ mountain in the world.   (high)

2 At 6741 kilometres the River Nile is _____ river in the world.   (long)

3 With an area of over 69,000 square kilometres, Lake Victoria is _____ lake in Africa.   (big)

4 With their best-selling albums and hit singles, the Beatles were _____ British pop group in the 1960s.   (successful)

5 The Pacific is _____ and _____ ocean in the world, at over 165 million square miles and with an average depth of 4215 metres. (large, deep)

6 The whale is _____ mammal that exists.   (large)

7 The humming-bird is one of _____ birds we know of.   (small)

8 The cheetah, which has black spots and long legs, is _____ mammal on Earth.   (fast)

9 Antidisestablishmentarianism is supposed to be _____ word in the English language!   (long)

10 At 1343 metres Ben Nevis in the Grampian Mountains is _____ peak in Britain.   (high)

11 China has _____ population in the world – about 900 million. Some people say it is also _____ continuing civilisation. (large, old)

12 *Gone With The Wind* is one of _____ films ever made.   (popular)

13 Martina Navratilova was _____ woman tennis player of her time. (good)

14 Pollution is _____ problem in many towns today.   (bad)

15 The inventors of Esperanto, the world language, hoped it would become _____ way for people all round the world to communicate. (easy)

UNIT 20

Recycling

A Complete the sentences with the correct preposition.

1 He comes _____ China and speaks Mandarin.

2 They arrived _____ the main railway station _____ Stockholm _____ three o'clock.

3 I've never been _____ the United States, but I have been _____ South America.

4 Susan's piano teacher lives very _____ here, _____ 32 Green Lane.

5 He arrived _____ work _____ 9.30 _____ the morning.

6 We decided to travel _____ bicycle, take a tent and camp _____ nights.

7 They work _____ Singapore, but every summer they have a long holiday _____ Europe.

8 Can you see my village _____ the map? It's just there, _____ the middle.

9 Do you like that photo? It was taken _____ my uncle, who is a photographer.

10 We could go _____ the cinema tonight, or go _____ a fast food place _____ a hamburger, or go _____ a walk. What do you think?

11 My cousin lives _____ Pisa, which is quite _____ Florence.

12 I'll meet you _____ the National Gallery. It's _____ Trafalgar Square, you know. _____ there we can easily get a bus _____ Victoria Station.

13 He was born _____ a Tuesday, _____ six o'clock _____ the morning _____ 30th January 1776.

14 _____ New Year's Eve people often go _____ parties and celebrate the end of the old year. Then _____ New Year's Day there are football matches and other sporting events to go _____ .

15 I'm hoping to arrive _____ Manchester Airport early _____ the morning. I'm only going _____ a short business trip, so I expect to be back _____ the weekend.

16 Stuart always plays tennis _____ summer, but _____ winter he only plays hockey.

17 Put the toys _____ the cupboard, please, and the dirty clothes _____ the washing machine. And I don't want that pile of books _____ the table!

18 My house is _____ the school, so I usually walk home _____ the evening.

B Complete the second sentence so that it has a similar meaning to the first one. Use no more than **three** words.

1 My homework takes a long time, but yours doesn't.

Your homework doesn't _____ as mine.

2 The company gave Miss Harrison a gold watch when she left.

Miss Harrison _____ a gold watch when she left the company.

3 I advise you to be more truthful in future.

If I were you, _____ more truthful in future.

4 We live quite near the school, but Harry does[...]

Harry lives _____ the school[...]

5 The last time he flew a plane was in 2002.

He _____ a plane since 200[...]

6 Maria isn't as tall as her sister.

Maria's sister is _____ is.

7 The police found some very clear fingerpr[...]

Some very clear fingerprints _____ on [...]

8 You drink more coffee than Paul.

Paul doesn't _____ coffee as you do.

C Match the two halves of the conditional sentences. Use each item only once.

1 I wouldn't accept the job   A   if it's run out of paper.

2 What would you do   B   if he remembers.

3 I could help you with the shopping   C   if they want to buy a house.

4 We'll give you a call   D   unless they find suitable food.

5 The machine won't print anything   E   unless she changes her mind before then.

6 He'll pass on the message   F   if you'd like me to.

7 We'll go to Scotland   G   if I were you.

8 People usually put down a large deposit   H   if we visit Beirut.

9 She'll be there in two weeks   I   if you lost your purse?

10 In winter, small birds die   J   if we can afford the train fare.

D Complete the story, putting **one** word in each space.

My cousin Catherine used to go to 1) _____ very smart private boarding school for girls. In the Easter holidays, she came home to her family's big old farmhouse in the country as usual. Then, 2) _____ 1st April, a letter arrived for Catherine. Her mother, my Aunt Eileen, 3) _____ it to her at breakfast. When Catherine opened it, she looked shocked. 'Oh no!' she cried. 'My best friend from school, Lucy, 4) _____ coming here today! She says she's arriving on the 3 o'clock train! Oh, how awful! Look, Mum! Just look at the house!' It was true that things were untidier 5) _____ usual. There was a 6) _____ of dust on the furniture, and the floors were dirty.

Aunt Eileen sighed. 'Yes, I've 7) _____ so busy lately, and you haven't done much housework either, have you?'

'I've only got six hours! Where's the hoover?' said Catherine, rushing out of the room. And 8) _____ the next few hours, Aunt Eileen sat back and watched. Catherine cleaned, dusted, hoovered, polished, and 9) _____ flowers in the vases. She even baked a cake for tea.

But finally, 10) _____ 2.30 p.m., just as Catherine was sinking exhausted into a chair, Aunt Eileen looked happily round the sparkling house and said, 'April Fool, dear! I wrote the letter 11) _____ . Rather a good one, wasn't it? I must say, the house looks *wonderful*. You're much 12) _____ at cleaning than I thought.'

UNIT 21

Easily confused verbs

Lend: • *Can you lend me your dictionary for a moment?*
Borrow: • *Can I borrow your pencil-sharpener, please?*

Come, bring (for movement towards the speaker):
• *They came into the room where we were waiting, and brought the dog with them.*

Go, take (for movement away from the speaker):
• *When you go home, take a present for your mother.*

Be used to -ing (a present habit, a change from the past):
• *Now I'm in England, I'm used to driving on the left – I'd never done that before.*
Used to (a past habit):
• *We used to play tennis every day when we were at school.*

A Complete the sentences with verbs from the study box.

1 May I _____ your hairdryer after supper?

2 Hey! _____ over here and see what I've found!

3 My grandfather _____ to smoke, but he gave up two years ago.

4 There's something wrong with this new radio. I'm going to _____ it back to the shop.

5 If you _____ me £5, I promise to pay it back tomorrow.

6 We asked the waiter to _____ us some coffee.

7 It seemed strange at first, but now I'm quite _____ to having dinner late.

8 When you leave here, _____ straight ahead and then turn right.

B Match the phrases 1–6 with the correct ending, A or B.

1 Can I ____
2 May I ____
3 Can you ____   A borrow your bike?
4 Is it OK if I ____   B lend me your pen?
5 Do you mind if I ____
6 Will you please ____

C Underline the correct alternative in the sentences.

1 Do *come / go* to my party, and *bring / take* all your friends with you!

2 Anita's really kind – she *borrowed / lent* me her laptop.

3 Before Ahmed bought his car, he used to *walking / walk* to the office.

4 I never want to see you again! *Come / Go* away, and *bring / take* all your things with you!

5 Now that they live in Australia, the whole family is used to *spend / spending* most of the time in the open air.

6 I must remember to *take / bring* my ID card when I *come / go* to the disco on Saturday.

Adjectives and adverbs

Adjectives describe a noun or pronoun, often with **be**:
- She's very healthy.   • He's an excellent businessman.

Adverbs describe a verb: • The train moved slowly out of the station.
or can be used to describe an **adjective**:
- It was a well cooked meal.   • It was an extremely funny joke.

Most **adverbs** are made by adding **-ly** to an **adjective**:
- warm ~ warmly   • beautiful ~ beautifully   • sad ~ sadly
but note these spelling changes: • angry ~ angrily   • terrible ~ terribly
and these exceptions: • hard ~ hard   • fast ~ fast   • good ~ well

Notice these two types of **adjectives**, ending in **-ed**: • I was interested in his story.
and ending in **-ing**: • The programme was thrilling.   • What a fascinating idea!

A Decide if you need an adjective or an adverb in the sentences, and write ADJ or ADV in the spaces.

Then supply an adjective or adverb for each space.

1 He's a very ____ man.
2 She's so ____ , isn't she?
3 Drive ____ , can't you!
4 He's got a ____ house.
5 They worked ____ , didn't they?
6 It was a ____ simple plan.
7 ____ she turned round.
8 Oh, I'm so ____ sorry!
9 I broke her ____ cup.
10 You ____ offered to help me.

B Choose the correct word from the pair in brackets to complete the sentences.

1 We were _____ by the film.   (thrilled / thrilling)
2 It was a really _____ story.   (amused / amusing)
3 The office manager was very _____ in computers.
   (interested / interesting)
4 I went to sleep because the film was so _____ .   (bored / boring)
5 Such a _____ programme! I really enjoyed it.
   (fascinated / fascinating)

Although **adverbs** are usually used to describe verbs, some verbs (**appear, feel, look, seem, smell, sound, taste**) take an **adjective** when describing the subject:
- That sounds wonderful!   • Doesn't she look cheerful?
and an **adverb** when describing the action: • She tasted the sauce carefully.

C Complete the sentences with the correct form of the word in brackets.

1 Stephen spoke _____ to his brother.   (quiet)
2 Andreas always drives _____ on motorways.   (fast)
3 Julia's cooking usually tastes _____ .   (delicious)
4 Don't trust him; he sounds _____ , but I don't think he is.
   (honest)
5 My neighbour looked _____ at me over the fence.   (angry)

More adverbs

Always, **usually / normally / generally**, **often**, **sometimes**, **rarely / seldom**, **never** are adverbs of frequency, which usually go between the subject and the verb:
- *She often drinks tea.*   • *They never arrive late.*

or between the two parts of a verb:
- *I've seldom seen him.*   • *Do you often come here?*

Long adverbs / adverb phrases, including **very much**, usually go at the end of a sentence:
- *He learnt the poem by heart.*   • *I like cheese, cherries and chocolate very much!*

Time adverbs usually go at the beginning or end of a sentence:
- *She'll come tomorrow.*   • *Last year we had a great time.*
- *Suddenly there was a loud bang.*

Adverbs like **really**, **almost**, **hardly** usually go just before the words they refer to:
- *She's really intelligent.*   • *He's almost twenty-one.*
- *She has hardly any friends.*

A Put the adverbs given in a suitable place in the sentences.

1 We heard a crash. — SUDDENLY
2 She likes strawberries and cream. — VERY MUCH
3 We go shopping in the afternoon. — SOMETIMES
4 I think he washes his hair. — TWICE A WEEK
5 We have seen him waiting at the bus stop. — OFTEN
6 We go to school. — EVERY DAY
7 I'm hoping to get a letter. — TOMORROW
8 She takes her dog for a walk after breakfast. — USUALLY
9 He walked down the street. — VERY SLOWLY
10 Could you ask him to come? — AS SOON AS POSSIBLE
11 He accepted the job. — IMMEDIATELY
12 She drinks coffee in the evening. — NEVER
13 We had to learn the grammar rules. — BY HEART
14 Nobody studied hard enough. — LAST YEAR
15 I have eaten such tasty rice. — SELDOM

B Put the words in the right order to make correct sentences, making sure that the adverbs are in the right position.

1 the Frankfurt go we to theatre in sometimes
2 well children behaved extremely the
3 likes much the rain she very walking in
4 day Adam homework every his does
5 never they Cairo been have to
6 you park the jog round often do?
7 postcard yesterday him sent a I
8 on will there time be they?

9 never her car has he driven new

10 often headaches you do have?

11 extremely he to spoke me kindly

12 the arrived scene suddenly car

13 new last they computer week

14 happily his he down to sat

Too: • *The soup was too*

Enough: • *She wasn't old enough to enter university.* • *He didn't have enough money to go on holiday.*

Already (for positive sentences), **yet** (for questions and negative):
• *Have you done your work yet?* • *I haven't been to the post office yet.*
• *I've already cleaned my room.*

Still: • *I've been waiting for an hour, and I'm still waiting!* • *Is he still working in Chicago?* • *I still haven't received the money.*

Hardly: • *I hardly speak any Russian.* (= I speak very little Russian.)
• *She hardly ever comes here.* (= almost never)

C Match the parts of the sentences. Use each item only once.

1	The fried food was	A	too young	a	to eat.
2	The boy was	B	too difficult	b	to learn.
3	Lara didn't run	C	enough snow	c	to catch the bus.
4	The vocabulary was	D	enough money	d	to hold the toy.
5	Sadly, we haven't got	E	too expensive	e	to join the army.
6	I'm sure there'll be	F	too small	f	to buy a sports car.
7	The child's hand was	G	too greasy	g	for us to ski.
8	The flat was nice, but	H	fast enough	h	for us to rent.

D Complete the sentences with one of the following adverbs:
already hardly still yet

1 Why are you _____ here? Everybody else has gone home.

2 I _____ ever see my neighbours. They go away a lot.

3 Have you renewed your passport _____ ? No? Well, I've _____ renewed mine!

4 We've written to the tax office three times, and they _____ haven't replied!

5 Charlie has a wonderful job. He _____ does any work at all!

6 Don't bother about the front door. I've _____ locked it.

7 Can't you give me the answer _____ ? I've asked you twice!

8 We're _____ hoping to arrive in time, but I'm not sure we will.

9 He _____ speaks any French, so he doesn't understand Jacques.

10 She's _____ sent some faxes, checked her inbox and gone to lunch!

11 He's _____ in love with her, although he doesn't see her any more.

12 I'm so sorry, I haven't e-mailed the photos _____ . I'll do it today.

Gerund and infinitive

A **gerund** is the **-ing** form of a verb acting as a noun. We use it after certain verbs (like **love, enjoy, hate, avoid, mind**) and all prepositions:
- *He never minds helping people.* • *She's very fond of reading novels.*

We also use it as a subject:
- *Swimming is good for you.* • *Getting up early can be difficult.*

A Complete the sentences with the gerund of the following verbs:
help repair take type walk watch

1 The girls next door always enjoy _____ old films.
2 _____ exercise is recommended by health experts.
3 My uncle is keen on _____ veteran cars.
4 Are you good at _____ ? How many words a minute?
5 I'm a bit afraid of _____ home alone in the dark.
6 Would you mind _____ me with the shopping?

An **infinitive** is the basic form of the verb, with or without **to**. We use it *with* **to** after many verbs (**want, would like, decide, ought, hope, promise, offer, manage**): • *I decided to apply for the job at once.*
We use it *without* **to** after most modal verbs (**must, can, may, might, should**), and **let** and **make**: • *She never lets me help her.*
- *You can drive there.*

B Complete the sentences, using the correct form of the verb in brackets.

1 We managed _____ the car that we wanted. (buy)
2 I think you should _____ her some flowers. (give)
3 Bill's parents won't let him _____ to the party. (go)
4 We must _____ to the invitation at once. (reply)
5 They would really like _____ the art gallery on Friday. (visit)
6 Those boys might _____ the football club this season. (join)
7 Did the teacher make you _____ your homework? (finish)
8 The actress was hoping _____ a part in the new play. (get)

C Match the two halves of the sentences. Use each item only once.

1 Sven is keen   A to close down the factory.
2 We don't mind   B deliver the letter tomorrow.
3 The boss has decided   C to turn her palace into a hospital.
4 The whole family enjoys   D to share his ice cream.
5 The postman may   E in collecting old books?
6 The little boy offered   F reading detective stories.
7 Victoria is very good   G on finding a new job.
8 Are you interested   H at keeping out of trouble.
9 The princess promised   I waiting for you for ten minutes.

UNIT 25

Recycling

A Read the text and choose the correct word or phrase (A, B, C or D) for each space.

'The history of York is the history of England.' That's what King George VI 1) _____ about the city which 2) _____ lived through 2000 years of history. You can 3) _____ York on guided bus tours, on river cruises, or just by walking round 4) _____ old city walls.

5) _____ the Romans arrived in England, they made York an important centre 6) _____ people studied, worked and lived. In the Middle Ages there was more building, as you 7) _____ see from the old wooden houses and narrow streets. Perhaps the people of York are most proud of their wonderful cathedral, the Minster, which can be 8) _____ from almost everywhere in the city.

Today there 9) _____ museums and churches to visit; there are also lots of cafés and restaurants, so I promise you 10) _____ leave York hungry!

	A	B	C	D
1	say	told	said	tells
2	has	have	had	having
3	visiting	to visit	visitor	visit
4	the	a	an	some
5	While	When	Because	Before
6	where	which	who	whose
7	must	could	can	cannot
8	seeing	saw	see	seen
9	is	are	were	was
10	won't	will	aren't	going to

B Match the phrases 1–15 with the correct form of *drive*.

1 You ought ____
2 He's fond ____
3 They're good ____
4 Please let me ____
5 We always enjoy ____
6 Don't make him ____
7 I don't mind ____
8 She's keen ____
9 You're afraid ____
10 I've decided ____
11 You should ____
12 We must ____
13 They used ____
14 She's now used ____
15 She's always wanted ____

A drive.
B to drive.
C to driving.
D at driving.
E on driving.
F driving.
G of driving.

C Choose the correct word(s) from the pair in brackets to complete the sentences.

1 Can you possibly _____ me a little money? (lend / borrow)

2 He shouted _____ at the children. (angry / angrily)

3 Are you _____ waiting to see the doctor? (yet / still)

4 Excuse me! Could you _____ the menu over here, please? (bring / take)

5 We were very tired because we'd worked so _____ all day. (hard / hardly)

6 The driver only just avoided _____ the parked car. (hit / hitting)

7 I'm not used to _____ up early! (get / getting)

8 We _____ do our shopping at the market. (often / every day)

D Complete the second sentence so that it has a similar meaning to the first one. Use no more than **three** words.

1 We didn't have enough money to buy the skis.

The skis were too _____ to buy.

2 This soup has a really delicious taste, doesn't it?

This soup tastes _____ , doesn't it?

3 He only has a few words of Portuguese.

He can hardly _____ Portuguese.

4 It would be a nice idea to send him a card.

I think you _____ a card.

5 Michaela was too short to reach the top shelf.

Michaela wasn't _____ reach the top shelf.

6 In my view, she's a very good tennis player.

She plays tennis _____ , in my opinion.

7 I want to invite you to my party.

Would you like _____ to my party?

8 I loved the film. I was fascinated by it – weren't you?

What a great film! It was _____ , wasn't it?

9 Didn't your aunt let you go out last night?

Did your aunt make you _____ last night?

10 We've seldom seen him here.

We haven't _____ seen him here.

11 I don't like Tim because he's so selfish.

If Tim weren't so selfish, _____ him.

12 The exam was more difficult than I expected.

The exam wasn't _____ I expected.

13 Winning the competition would mean I'd become famous.

If I _____ the competition, I'd become famous.

14 The police arrested the company director last week.

The company director _____ last week.

15 Perhaps nobody else wants the job, so I might apply for it.

If nobody else wants the job, _____ for it.

Have something done

> **Have something done** is used when you ask someone to do something for you, and you often pay them to do it:
> • *I must have my hair cut soon.*   • *He needs to have his suits cleaned.*
>
> Use the verb *have*, the object and the past participle of the verb you need.
> (The past participle is the third part of the verb form: *done* from *do, did, done.*)
> **Remember** to keep this word order – 1) *have* 2) *something* 3) *done.*

A Match the numbers with the letters to make suitable sentences. Use each item only once.

I'm having

1	the car	A installed.
2	the kitchen	B copied.
3	the living-room carpet	C serviced.
4	my hair	D cleaned.
5	the piano	E cut and restyled.
6	my shoes	F decorated.
7	air conditioning	G mended.
8	the video of the birthday party	H tuned.

B Your friend Camilla has a lot of problems, and is asking you for advice, because she isn't very good at solving them! When she tells you about them, give her your suggestions, starting with *I think you should have ... (something done)* or *Why don't you have ... (something done?).*

1 Our house really needs painting, but I can't do it myself! What's your advice?

2 The grass in the garden is so long! What shall I do?

3 My hair looks awful, doesn't it? Should I try a different colour, or style?

4 I spilt some milk on these trousers yesterday. Oh, dear, they do look dirty!

5 We can't watch the news this evening. The television just isn't working any more. What shall I do about it?

6 I really want to look good for Sue's wedding, but I can't find a nice dress in the shops. And I'm no good at dressmaking myself. What can I do?

7 Brrh! Isn't it cold in here! There's no fire in this room at all. We really need central heating, don't we?

8 Our car broke down the other day. I wonder if someone should check it before we take it overland to India? We're leaving next week. What do you think?

9 Just look at my shoe! The heel fell off yesterday! I can't wear it like that. What shall I do?

10 The piano sounds strange, doesn't it? Is there anything wrong with it? What do you think I should do about it?

11 Someone spilt a pot of coffee over that white carpet last week. Doesn't it look terrible! What can I do?

12 Look, one of the legs has come off the kitchen table. It's no good at all like that. Have you any idea what I should do about it?

Reported speech

Reported speech is used, often with **say**, and sometimes with **tell** + object, to report to a third person what was said earlier: • *'I feel better.'* ~ *What did he say? ~ He said (that) he felt better. / He told me (that) he felt better.*

Normally, the tense, the pronoun and the time phrase are changed in **reported speech**:
Direct statement: • *'I am leaving tomorrow,' he said.*
Reported statement: • *He said (that) he was leaving the next day.*

Direct	Reported	Direct	Reported
am / is / are	was / were	tomorrow	the next day / the day after
has / have	had	today	that day
does / walks	did / walked	yesterday	the day before
was	had been	ago	before
did	had done	here	there
will	would		
can	could		

A What did he say? Put these simple statements into reported speech. Start with *He said (that) ...* or *He told me (that) ... .*

1 'My name's Pablo.'
2 'I live in Austria.'
3 'I've got a brother and a sister.'
4 'My father is a manager.'
5 'My mother works in a bank.'
6 'I'm a very sociable person.'
7 'I like pop music.'
8 'My best subject is history.'
9 'I walk to school every day.'
10 'I can swim very fast.'

B What did he / she / they say? Put these more difficult statements into reported speech.

1 'I'll be there by 2 o'clock,' Sarah said.
2 'Tony always works very hard,' said Michael.
3 'I think she eats too much chocolate,' said Patrick.
4 'We'll help you if we can,' said the two men.
5 'I don't feel very well,' said Betty.
6 'I'm going to the dentist tomorrow,' said Liz.
7 'I'm sure I can finish it in time,' said Anna.
8 'You've all done very well in the test,' said the teacher.

Reported commands use **tell** and the infinitive:
• *'Go home!' ~ He told me to go home.*
• *'Don't wait. ' ~ He told me not to wait.*

or **ask**, for a politer command, or request:
• *'Please don't talk any more.' ~ She asked us not to talk any more.*
• *'Can I see the manager?' ~ He asked to see the manager.*

C Look at the situations. What happened next? Complete the reported commands or requests, using no more than **three** words.

1 The students were talking loudly in the classroom. Suddenly the teacher came in.

The teacher told _____ stop talking.

2 John wanted to park his car outside the hospital, but a policeman came along.

The policeman told him _____ there.

3 A girl was trying to carry some very heavy books. She met a friend.

She asked her friend _____ with the books.

4 There was no bread in the house, but your parents were very busy.

They asked you _____ bread on your way home.

5 I often phone my friend late at night, but one day he said to me, 'My parents don't like it when people phone very late.'

He asked me _____ late at night any more.

6 We were in the classroom when the teacher realised she had left a book in the library.

She asked one of us _____ from the library for her.

7 My friend borrowed some money from me. I really needed it.

I asked him _____ back to me as soon as possible.

8 I didn't do my homework, so I couldn't give it to the teacher.

The teacher told me _____ to him the next day.

Reported questions express direct questions beginning with or without a question word:
- *'Why are you here?' ~ She asked why I was there.*
- *'Can you swim?' ~ She asked if I could swim.*

Note the word order: • *'Where **is the book**?' ~ She asked where **the book was**.*

D Match the direct questions with the reported questions. Use each item only once.

1 'Where are the toilets?'

2 'How long have you been here?'

3 'What's your name?'

4 'Can you make an appointment?'

5 'Have you seen the new film?'

6 'Why aren't you in the top class?'

7 'Are you listening?'

8 'When does the office close?'

9 'Please can we come?'

10 'Please can I leave?'

A She asked what my name was.

B She asked if I'd seen the new film.

C I asked if I could leave.

D She asked why I wasn't in the top class.

E They asked how long we had been there.

F He asked if I could make an appointment.

G She asked when the office closed.

H They asked if they could come.

I He asked if I was listening.

J He asked where the toilets were.

Common phrasal verbs

A **phrasal verb** is a verb plus one, two, or even three prepositions, which has a special meaning that you cannot easily guess. So you need to learn each phrasal verb separately. Here are some very common ones:

break down	stop working	**look after**	take care of
call for	collect	**look up**	try to find information
find out	discover	**run out of**	have no more left
get on	make progress	**set off / out**	start a journey
get up	rise from bed	**sort out**	organise, solve a problem
give up	stop	**take off**	depart (plane)
grow up	become adult	**turn off**	stop, switch off
hold on	wait	**turn on**	start, switch on

A Complete the sentences with the correct phrasal verb from the study box.

1 I want to _____ where Sonia was yesterday. I'm going to ask her!

2 If you keep a pet, you must _____ it properly.

3 I don't know his phone number. I'll _____ it _____ in the phone book.

4 The files are untidy, so he is going to _____ them _____ .

5 What time does your plane _____ ?

6 Ooh, the film's about to start! Let's _____ the television, shall we?

7 What time shall I _____ you tonight? 8 o'clock?

8 Don't _____ now! Try again! You can do it!

B Match the statements or questions with the responses. Use each item only once.

1 Why were you so late?

2 When do you get up?

3 Where's the sugar?

4 This programme's very boring.

5 When are you setting off?

6 How are you getting on at school?

7 Can I speak to Tricia, please?

8 This exercise is too difficult.

9 Where did you spend your childhood?

10 How do you spell 'committee'?

A Sorry, we've run out of it.

B Early on Thursday morning.

C Shall we turn it off, then?

D Yes. Hold on a moment, please.

E My car broke down on the motorway.

F Try looking it up in the dictionary.

G I grew up in the south of France.

H Usually at about half past seven.

I Let's give up and have a cup of coffee.

J Quite well, thank you.

Linking words

Linking words connect parts of sentences. Here are some common ones:

And links two similar ideas. **But** links two different ideas:
• *She went to the party and had a lovely time.*   • *He worked in India and in Africa.*
• *She wanted to go on holiday, but did not have enough money.*

Either / or link alternatives: • *We could either go out or stay in.*

To / in order to show a purpose: • *He came to Arizona to study farming.*

Because shows a reason: • *They arrived late because the traffic was so heavy.*

As, **when**, **while**, **since**, **before**, **after**, **as soon as** show time:
• *The phone rang as I entered.*   • *He was counting the money while he was speaking.*   • *I've learnt a lot since I arrived.*   • *Come as soon as you can.*

So that / such ... that / so ... that show a result:
• *It seemed so difficult that she started crying.*   • *It was such hot coffee that he couldn't drink it.*   • *He sold his motorbike, so that he could pay for a holiday.*

Although links contrasting ideas:
• *I like maths, although I'm not very good at it.*

A Connect the following parts of sentences, using suitable words or phrases from the study box.

1 She was typing the report _____ her boss was dictating it.

2 He went to Mexico _____ learn Spanish.

3 I was angry with her _____ she was so rude to me.

4 There was _____ much snow _____ the roads became blocked.

5 We could _____ go to art classes, _____ practise Italian conversation. Which would you prefer?

6 It was _____ a long journey _____ everybody was very tired _____ the plane finally landed.

7 _____ he had lost his job, he still spent a lot of money on clothes.

8 I'd like to visit Loch Ness _____ see the monster, _____ it's too far to go for a weekend.

B Match the two halves of the sentences. Use each item only once.

1 Although I like her,   A because it was too difficult.

2 He drove so fast   B as soon as you find out.

3 We've lived here   C that we might have a swim.

4 I didn't do the work   D or revise for his exams.

5 Tell me the answer   E since the beginning of the year.

6 He asked her to marry him,   F but she didn't want to.

7 It's such a lovely day   G I think she's rather mean.

8 He'll either watch TV   H that he arrived by lunchtime.

Recycling

A Read the text and choose the correct word or phrase (A, B, C or D) for each space.

Maria Callas was the 1) _____ famous soprano of the postwar period. Born 2) _____ 1923, the Greek opera singer had a truly wonderful voice 3) _____ a passionate nature. She was known for 4) _____ technical skill and enthusiasm for hard work. She sang in all the world's great opera houses, 5) _____ her career was full of personal dramas. She was dismissed 6) _____ the manager of the Metropolitan Opera House in New York, in a famous personality conflict.

She had 7) _____ very public relationship with Aristotle Onassis in the late 1950s. Throughout her life her expensive tastes in clothes and her high-profile social life 8) _____ her a very public figure. Her final stage appearance 9) _____ as Tosca 10) _____ Covent Garden Opera House in 1965.

She spent her last years 11) _____ Paris, living very quietly and seeing 12) _____ any visitors. She died in 1977.

	A	B	C	D
1	most	more	less	least
2	at	on	in	by
3	so	and	than	since
4	the	his	hers	her
5	so that	but	because	when
6	of	with	by	from
7	the	a	a little	an
8	made	make	making	makes
9	were	is	are	was
10	at	on	in	about
11	on	at	in	round
12	few	hardly	not	no

B Match the two halves of the sentences. Use each item only once.

1 She's having	A to give them his passport.
2 The policeman told the driver	B his address in the office files.
3 Wendy asked	C I read the newspaper.
4 Would you mind	D two rooms decorated.
5 You could look up	E but she left early.
6 They asked Peter	F because it was too expensive.
7 Before I had lunch,	G that the road wasn't safe.
8 We didn't buy the clock,	H if I was going home later.
9 Why don't you have	I turning on the television?
10 She enjoyed the party,	J your curtains cleaned?

C Choose the correct word(s) from the pair in brackets to complete the sentences.

1 _____ she worked hard, she didn't pass the entry test. (Although / But)

2 He washed the dirty dishes _____ he had finished supper. (before / after)

3 We cleaned our boots _____ they were dirty. (because / while)

4 She saved a lot of money _____ she could go on an expensive holiday. (so that / but)

5 He bought a small house _____ painted it himself. (but / and)

6 The food smelt _____ good that we started eating at once. (such / so)

7 They went to London _____ see a musical. (to / as)

8 He's been in Brazil _____ he started work there last year. (for / since)

9 You can phone him _____ you get home. (as soon as / although)

10 He thought about his homework _____ he was having a bath. (while / and)

D Complete the second sentence so that it has a similar meaning to the first one. Use no more than **three** words.

1 'Don't open your exam papers!' he said.
He told us _____ our exam papers.

2 I'm going to ask Kevin to restyle my hair.
I'm having _____ by Kevin.

3 I'm sorry, we have no coffee left today.
I'm afraid we've run _____ today.

4 'I'll do the shopping today,' said Barbara.
Barbara said that _____ the shopping that day.

5 Are you making progress with your project?
How are you _____ with your project?

6 I'll collect you at 8.
I'll call _____ at 8.

7 'Can I see you tomorrow?' she asked.
She asked if she _____ the next day.

8 He may be here soon, and then he'll tell us the answer.
If he _____ , he'll tell us the answer.

9 I think you should get someone to fit a new kitchen in your flat.
Why don't you have a _____ in your flat?

10 My plane leaves at 12.20.
My plane takes _____ 12.20.

11 People who are in a hurry sometimes make mistakes.
Mistakes are sometimes _____ people who are in a hurry.

12 Costas would love to visit Canada, but he hasn't got enough money.
If Costas _____ , he could visit Canada.

Nouns

A **noun** can be a word for a person, place or thing you can see or touch. But there are also also **abstract nouns** for ideas like *peace, love, memory* and *happiness*.

Some common endings for abstract nouns are ignor**ance**, differ**ence**, suggest**ion**, rac**ism**, secur**ity,** arrange**ment**, good**ness**.
More unusual endings are wis**dom**, child**hood**, relation**ship**, leng**th**.
Other common abstract nouns are *anger, beauty, feeling, hope, humour, idea, luck, surprise* and *trust*.

(See **Unit 78** for help with irregular plurals and spelling of nouns, and **Unit 14** for countable and uncountable nouns.)

A Which nouns are abstract? Underline the abstract nouns in these sentences.

1 'Bad luck!' said Morgan, as I dropped my bag of sandwiches.
2 I made some wonderful friendships at school, and received an excellent education.
3 What an improvement! That child has now learnt to control his anger.
4 Gordon has a great sense of humour, which has helped him through many difficulties.
5 It was quite a surprise to see my mother on the doorstep.

B Complete the sentences with an abstract noun, using the correct form of the word in brackets.

1 I've always had a good _____ with my boss. (relation)
2 Writers often use their _____ in their work. (imagine)
3 She has no _____ who sent her the present! (idea)
4 Everyone likes him because of his _____ . (kind)
5 We stared at our teacher in _____ . (amaze)
6 I want to help, but in _____ it'll be difficult. (real)
7 'Darling, our _____ will last for ever!' he told her. (love)
8 There are several other children in the _____ . (neighbour)
9 The _____ of their welcome surprised me. (warm)
10 At last the prisoners were given their _____ . (free)

Most **compound nouns** are a combination of two nouns:
• *coffee cake* (a kind of cake, with coffee in it)
• *hotel room* (a room in a hotel)

The first noun is usually singular:
• *tourist office* (an office where tourists get information, NOT *tourists office*)
• *pet food* (food for pets)

Some common compounds are written as one word:
• *briefcase, guidebook, handwriting, headache, keyboard, lighthouse, teapot*

C Complete the compound nouns using the following words:
helicopter dish fish note tennis strawberry rock computer arm dinner guard car

1 _____ concert
2 _____ washer
3 _____ market
4 _____ plate
5 _____ chair
6 _____ dog
7 _____ key
8 _____ book
9 _____ ball
10 _____ jam
11 _____ pilot
12 _____ screen

D Change each phrase to make a compound noun.

1 a floor made of stones
2 an engineer who repairs televisions
3 a person who drives buses
4 a sign on the road
5 a belt to keep money in
6 service for customers
7 a museum in a town
8 a shop selling furniture
9 a machine which cleans by using a vacuum
10 oil made from olives

Possessives

We use **'s** to show that a noun belongs to just **one** person or animal:
* *the doctor's car*   • *the little boy's jeans*   • *the dog's ears*

Another common use of the possessive **'s** is when a noun has an irregular plural:
* *the children's supper*   • *people's mistakes*   • *a women's magazine*

We use **s'** to show that a noun belongs to **two or more** people or animals:
* *a walkers' guide*   • *my grandparents' village*   • *horses' hooves*

We sometimes say *a friend of mine* (= one of my friends), *an idea of his* (= one of his ideas), *a child of theirs* (= one of their children), *a project of yours* (= one of your projects).

Time words and names of days can be followed by **'s**:
* *tomorrow's weather*   • *Saturday's newspaper*

E Put these phrases into a different possessive form.

1 shoes for men
2 milk for the cat
3 a blue coat belonging to a girl
4 the house belonging to her parents
5 the neck of a giraffe
6 one of her letters
7 brushes that painters use
8 the menu for today
9 ideas that people have
10 a knife that a cook uses
11 the advice given by the doctor
12 one of your stories
13 the cry of a child
14 the palace of the Queen
15 clothes for children
16 the nest of a bird
17 the meeting on Tuesday
18 the uniforms of the soldiers
19 the success of the students
20 the hat of a chef

More prepositions

Some common **nouns** and their prepositions are:
advice on / about, cause of, difference between, help with, information on / about, need for, pride in, reason for, result of, solution to
- *What was the cause of the crash?*
- *There's no difference between them.*

Some common **adjectives** and their prepositions are:
afraid / frightened of, angry / annoyed with, bad / good at, bored with, crowded with, engaged / married / related to, full of, interested in, keen on, proud of, ready for, surprised at, tired of
- *Have you heard? Simon's engaged to Tracy!*
- *Come in, Mr Smith – the doctor's ready for you.*

Some common **verbs** and their prepositions are:
agree / disagree with, apologise for, ask for, depend on, hope for, laugh at, look at, look forward to, speak to / about, talk to / about, thank someone for, wait for
- *I'm sorry, I disagree with you.*   • *Wait for me!*
- *Why didn't you ask for some help with your bags?*

Note: *discuss, tell, phone* and *reach* usually take no preposition:
- *We discussed the problem, and the policeman told me to phone him when I reached home.*

A Match the two halves of the sentences. Use each item only once.

1 Did you speak
2 She takes great pride
3 We need some advice
4 I'm afraid I'm very bad
5 My cousin was annoyed
6 We're hoping
7 Were you laughing
8 Liz is married
9 More money? That depends
10 He's always been frightened

A on how to get there.
B at me just now?
C of dogs.
D in her family.
E with her son for being late.
F for better weather tomorrow.
G to a friend of yours, isn't she?
H to the headmaster about it?
I on my boss.
J at taking regular exercise.

These prepositions and expressions with prepositions have something to do with **time**:
at the beginning of, at the end of, at first, at last, during, in time for, on time

- *At the end of his speech some people laughed.*
- *At first I was slow at typing, but now I'm much faster.*
- *We reached the front of the queue at last.*
- *They had tennis lessons during the holidays.*
- *I only just finished my homework in time for the class.*
- *Arrive on time, or there'll be trouble!*

B Complete the sentences with the correct preposition.

1 Molly grew much thinner ____ her illness.
2 You'll never get to the station ____ time ____ the train!
3 ____ the end ____ the film the hero marries the girl.
4 I've managed to lose some weight ____ last!
5 You should make an effort to be ____ time – it's rude to make people wait.
6 Using the mouse is hard ____ first, but you soon get used to it.

Here are some more common prepositions and expressions with prepositions:
into, out of, by, with, like, because of, by means of, in love with, for sale

- *The boys ran in and out of the house, shouting happily.*
- *The rock star arrived at the castle by helicopter.*
- *Prepare the vegetables with a sharp knife.*
- *You're a shy, quiet person, like me.*
- *The picnic's been cancelled because of the bad weather.*
- *You can check your account online by means of a password.*
- *She's been in love with him for years.*
- *If this cottage is for sale, we'd like to buy it.*

C Some of the sentences are not correct. Tick (✔) the correct ones and rewrite the wrong ones.

1 She soon became bored of her new job.
2 My friends and I travelled round the island on motorbike.
3 Because of the computer breakdown, we couldn't get our tickets.
4 Duncan works in publishing, same like my brother.
5 Do you always agree with everybody you talk to?
6 At the last he's decided what to do.
7 I think Joanna is related with Madonna.
8 My laptop is on sale, if anyone's interested.
9 She cleaned the floor with a wet cloth.
10 Perhaps I'll go – it depends of the weather.
11 Be careful – I think you're falling in love for him!
12 We reached to the hotel in time for dinner.

More modal verbs

Could is used to talk about general ability and possibility in the past:
- *I could ride a horse when I was six.*
- *We couldn't see anything because it was too dark.*
or for polite requests: • *Could you tell me the time?*

Would is also used for polite requests:
- *Would you mind opening the door, please?* • *Would you pass me the bread?*

Have to is like *must*, and is used to show what must be done:
- *I can't come today. I have to go to the dentist.*
- *We had to be at the airport two hours before the flight.*

In the present tense, we often use **have got to** instead of *have to*:
- *I've got to see him!*

Need shows what is necessary:
- *He needs to take his medicine regularly.*

Don't have to / Don't need to / Needn't are all ways of saying what isn't necessary: • *You don't have to wait.* • *We don't need to be there until six.*
- *He needn't come if he doesn't want to.*

Remember that **should** is often used for advice:
- *I think you should tell your friend your secret.*
And so is **would**, like this:
- *If I were you, I'd (= I would) go straight to the police.*

A Match the two halves of the sentences. Use each item only once.

1	If I were you,	A	leave yet.
2	We don't have to	B	go to bed if you feel so ill.
3	What time have we got to	C	helping me with this?
4	I think you should	D	check out of the hotel?
5	Would you mind	E	read by the age of three.
6	I remember that I could	F	I'd try and save some money.

B There is a mistake in all these sentences. A word is missing, or you need to remove a word, or use a different one. Correct the sentences.

1 That's a difficult situation – I think you would get some help.

2 Have you show me how to use the photocopier, please?

3 You don't need drive so fast – there's no hurry.

4 I'll have got to take a taxi, if I want to get to the meeting on time.

5 We were angry because we would only answer half the questions in the test.

6 You don't have got to do it, but it's a good idea.

7 If I were you, you wouldn't leave school at sixteen.

8 Don't be unhappy! You would try and look on the bright side of life.

9 Harry needn't to do this homework – he's already done more than the rest of you!

10 Should you give me a hand with the sofa, please? I can't lift it.

Verbs and objects

A common structure in English is **verb** + **object** + **infinitive** (usually with **to**):
- *I want you to listen.*
- *I'd like you to apply for the job.*
- *They allowed him to leave hospital.*

Notice that **make** and **let** are not followed by *to*, in active sentences:
- *The teachers made Isabel work hard.*
- *My brother let me use his car.*

Many verbs, like **bring**, **give**, **hand**, **lend**, **take**, **teach**, **send**, **show** can have two objects, a direct one and an indirect one. The indirect object usually refers to a person, and we usually put it first:
- *The waiter brought us the menu.* (instead of *... brought the menu to us.*)
- *I showed Jamie my new DVDs.* (instead of *I showed my new DVDs to Jamie.*)

Note that when we put the indirect object second, it normally has the preposition **to**:
- *The judge awarded the prize to the Russian singer.*

If both objects are personal pronouns, however, the direct object usually comes first:
- *Give it to me.*   • *Take them to her.*

A Some of the sentences are not correct. Tick (✔) the correct ones, and rewrite the wrong ones.

1 My mother didn't want that I go to college.
2 The officer manager let me to go home early.
3 Tell Douglas to come and see me, will you?
4 They don't allow that students use mobile phones in class.
5 I persuaded Portia to come to the cinema with me.
6 I'd like someone to explain the matter to me.
7 We didn't ask that you cleaned our car.
8 His wife reminded him to lock the door.
9 The captain ordered that his men march on.
10 I'd prefer that you book a table for 7.30, not 8 p.m.

B Put the words in the right order to make correct sentences.

1 letter postman the me handed the
2 money can some I lend you
3 bill me as possible send can as the you soon?
4 him useful I taught maths a of bit
5 present a him bought nice really we
6 took some birthday flowers her I for her
7 at show to it me once!
8 can it them give tomorrow you to

Recycling

A Read the text and choose the correct word or phrase (A, B, C or D) for each space.

In the churchyard at Bamburgh, a small town on the north-east coast of England, 1)_____ is a monument which 2)_____ designed to be seen 3)_____ any passing ship. It is to the 4)_____ of Grace Darling, the world's 5)_____ lifeboat heroine. Grace was 6)_____ in Bamburgh in 1815. She lived with her father William in the Longstone 7)_____ on the Farne Islands, a wild and windy place in the North Sea, where William 8)_____ to keep the light shining, to warn sailors of danger. 9)_____ 7th September 1838, the 23-year-old girl and her father 10)_____ their small boat 11)_____ the water, and rowed for over a kilometre through stormy seas to save nine sailors from the ship *SS Forfarshire*, which 12)_____ rocks on the Farne Islands and broken up. 13)_____ of her bravery, Grace became famous throughout England, but 14)_____ she died of a serious illness only three years later, and was buried in Bamburgh churchyard.

	A	B	C	D
1	it	there	actually	their
2	were	will be	had	was
3	with	on	by	for
4	love	trust	hope	memory
5	greatest	most great	greater	great
6	borne	birthday	born	birth
7	lighthouse	summerhouse	greenhouse	guesthouse
8	must	ought	could	had
9	In	On	At	While
10	have put	put	had put	were putting
11	into	out of	through	over
12	did hit	has hit	had hit	have hit
13	Because	In spite	Due	For reason
14	unlucky	pity	unhappy	sadly

B Underline the correct word or words to complete each sentence.

1 I think you *should* / *would* try learning another language.

2 Have you any information *in* / *on* recent snowfalls?

3 Let's *discuss* / *discuss about* this calmly and sensibly.

4 I entered the flat by *means* / *use* of a secret key.

5 Your new bike? You can show *it to me* / *me to it* tomorrow.

6 I'd like *that you* / *you to* explain why you're late.

7 If it's a *war's* / *war* film, I don't want to see it.

8 Don't worry, you *needn't* / *don't need* give me the money yet.

9 It was ten o'clock by the time we *reached to* / *reached* the airport.

10 Tom's always been a good *friendship* / *friend* to me.

C Complete the second sentence so that it has a similar meaning to the first one. Use no more than **three** words.

1 Please sit down and pay attention.

I want _____ sit down and pay attention, please.

2 It isn't necessary to buy him a present.

You don't _____ buy him a present.

3 Andrew wouldn't lend me his car.

Andrew didn't allow_____ his car.

4 If I were you, I'd buy a new modem.

In my opinion, you _____ buy a new modem.

5 In the end the prisoners were set free.

The prisoners were given their _____ in the end.

6 Those books are intended for children.

Those are _____ books.

7 Do we know what caused the accident?

What was _____ the accident?

8 I think Russell is Tamsin's husband.

I think Russell is _____ Tamsin.

9 She used a wooden spoon to stir the soup.

She stirred the soup _____ a wooden spoon.

10 All our information was given to him.

We _____ all our information.

D Complete the sentences with the correct prepositions.

1 I'm surprised ____ you, failing your exam like that. I thought you were good ____ maths!

2 Dolly's parents are angry ____ her, because she's just told them she's engaged ____ Kevin. She says she's ____ love ____ him!

3 I'll wait ____ you outside the cinema, then. Try and get there ____ time ____ the start of the film!

4 ____ the end ____ the book I couldn't stop crying – it was such a sad story. I suppose I wasn't ready ____ such a sad ending.

5 Ask your boss ____ a meeting. Say you want to talk ____ him. Just stay calm and don't show you're annoyed ____ him.

6 I always make sure I arrive ____ time. Wait a minute, what are you all laughing ____ ?

7 I've got a job interview tomorrow. I'm a bit frightened ____ giving wrong answers, but I'll just have to hope ____ the best.

8 I couldn't agree ____ you more! People have no pride ____ their work these days.

9 Happiness shouldn't depend ____ how much money you have.

10 Unfortunately I was ill ____ my holiday because ____ the heat.

Nationalities, countries and continents

> Make adjectives for countries and continents like this:
>
> with **-ese**: *Burmese, Chinese, Japanese, Maltese, Portuguese, Vietnamese*
>
> with **-i**: *Bangladeshi, Iraqi, Israeli, Kuwaiti, Pakistani, Yemeni*
>
> with **-n**, **-an** or **-ian**: *African, American, Argentinian, Asian, Australian, Austrian, Belgian, Brazilian, Canadian, Egyptian, European, German, Hungarian, Indian, Italian, Korean, Mexican, Norwegian, Peruvian, Russian*
>
> with **-ic**: *Arabic, Icelandic*
>
> with **-ish**: *British, Danish, Finnish, Irish, Scottish, Spanish, Swedish, Turkish*
>
> **Exceptions**: *Cypriot, Czech, Dutch, French, Greek, Swiss, Thai, Welsh*

A Find the correct nationality adjective from the study box for each country.

1 Switzerland
2 Malta
3 the Netherlands
4 China
5 Iraq

6 Iceland
7 the United States
8 Turkey
9 Greece
10 Portugal

11 Denmark
12 Thailand
13 Wales
14 Kuwait
15 Japan

B Test your general knowledge. What nationality is / was ...?

1 Marie Curie
2 Joan of Arc
3 Salvador Dali
4 Nelson Mandela
5 Michelangelo Buonarroti

6 Wolfgang Amadeus Mozart
7 Confucius
8 James Joyce
9 Cleopatra
10 Diego Maradona

11 Socrates
12 Marilyn Monroe
13 Karl Marx
14 Mahatma Gandhi
15 Catherine the Great

C Complete the sentences with the correct country or nationality.

1 I'm Indian; I come from _____ .

2 I'm Italian; I'm from _____ .

3 I'm Irish; I come from _____ .

4 I'm French; I'm from _____ .

5 I'm Scottish; I come from _____ .

6 I'm from the Czech Republic. I'm _____ .

7 I'm Taiwanese; I come from _____ .

8 I'm from Bangladesh. I'm _____ .

9 I'm Brazilian; I come from _____ .

10 I'm South Korean; I'm from _____ .

OVER TO YOU

What's your nationality? Where do you come from?

Which countries would you like to visit?

What nationality is your favourite sportsperson or pop star?

UNIT 37

Homes and furniture

terraced   semi-detached   detached   flat / apartment   block of flats
house   cottage   villa   bungalow   palace   ground floor   first floor
attic   basement   cellar   front door   back door   conservatory

She went upstairs to her bedroom on the first floor.
I live next door to my best friend.

A Choose the correct word from the pair in brackets to complete the sentences.

1 My grandmother lives in a _____ now, because she can't climb stairs any more. (bungalow / cottage)

2 If we go to Cyprus in the summer, we could rent a holiday _____ . (palace / apartment)

3 My room's very high up. It's in the _____ . (basement / attic)

4 Henry's father keeps all his wine in the _____ . (ground / cellar)

5 Lilian lives in a _____ house, with a big garden all round. (terraced / detached)

sofa	chair	fridge	bed
armchair	table	freezer	chest of drawers
lamp	desk	cooker	cupboard
television	computer	oven	wardrobe
video recorder	bookshelf	microwave	
stereo	bookcase	sink	bath
CD / DVD player	curtains	washing machine	shower
fireplace	blinds	dishwasher	(wash)basin
stool	rug	worktop	toilet

B Write down the item of furniture or piece of equipment that you need in these situations.

1 You want to put your smart suit away. Go to the _____ .

2 You need to keep milk cold. Put it in the _____ .

3 You want to find a detective story to read. Look on the _____ .

4 You want to watch the news. Switch on the _____ .

5 You want to relax in front of the TV. Sit on the _____ .

6 You need a teapot. Look in the _____ in the kitchen.

7 You need to wash a lot of cups and plates. Put them in the _____ .

8 It's getting dark in the room. Switch on the _____ .

OVER TO YOU

What type of building do you live in?

What furniture is there in your room?

What equipment is there in your kitchen?

UNIT 38

Days and dates

> **Months of the year**: *January, February, March, April, May, June, July, August, September, October, November, December*
>
> **Days of the week**: *Monday, Tuesday, Wednesday, Thursday, Friday, Saturday, Sunday*
>
> **Holidays**: *New Year's Day* (1st January), *Good Friday, Easter Sunday, Bank Holiday, Christmas Eve* (24th December), *Christmas Day* (25th December), *Boxing Day* (26th December), *New Year's Eve* (31st December)
>
> **Dates** are written like this: *1st 2nd 3rd 4th 5th*, etc.
> You can **write**: *25.5.97* or *25/5/97* or *25th May 1997* or *May 25th 1997*, but you **say**: **the** *twenty-fifth of May 1997*, or *May* **the** *twenty-fifth 1997*.

A Answer the questions about days and dates.

1 Today is Sunday. Mary left home the day before yesterday, and arrived in Geneva the same day. She's staying at her aunt's house there for three nights, then she's going on to Rome. After two nights in Rome, staying with her brother, she'll probably fly home.

What day did Mary arrive in Geneva? What day is she going to leave Geneva? What day will she probably fly home?

2 On December 30th 2004, Roy is still 18, but in 2005 he is 20. What date is his birthday, and what special name do we give this day?

3 When do people give each other presents in your country? When do families celebrate together, with a specially prepared meal?

4 When do many people promise themselves they will do better in future?

B Correct the following written dates.

1 97.5.30	_____	6 the 8th of December	_____
2 31th January	_____	7 1999, 2nd July	_____
3 3.27.98	_____	8 March the 10	_____
4 9/17/01	_____	9 the 1. April	_____
5 84.11.22	_____	10 20, 2, 52	_____

C Match the famous people with their dates of birth.

1 William Shakespeare   A July 102 BC

2 Guglielmo Marconi   B 16th December 1770

3 Ludwig van Beethoven   C 1st July 1961

4 Julius Caesar   D 25th April 1874

5 Princess Diana   E 23rd April 1564

OVER TO YOU

What festivals or public holidays do you have in your country?

What is your date of birth?

Clothes and fashion

fashionable	silk	(a pair of) jeans	sweater /	hat	shoes	dark
trendy	cotton	(a pair of) trousers	jumper	coat	boots	light
out-of-date	denim	(a pair of) shorts	cardigan	scarf	trainers	pale
smart	wool	suit	sweatshirt	gloves	flip-flops	striped
elegant	linen	jacket	fleece	collar	sandals	patterned
casual	polyester	waistcoat	T-shirt	sleeves	slippers	checked
	leather	tie	shirt	belt	high heels	plain
		dress	blouse	buttons	tights	long-sleeved
		skirt	swimsuit	earrings	socks	short-sleeved

She's size 12.   Can I try this on?   It fits you. (= It's the right size.)
It suits you. (= You look good in it.)   *It's made of polyester.*
The jacket goes with the skirt. (= The jacket matches the skirt.)

A Look at the people in the pictures and describe the clothes they are wearing, using words from the study box.

B Choose the correct word from the pair in brackets to complete the sentences.

1 What _____ shoes do you take? (size / number)

2 That colour really _____ you! (fits / suits)

3 Her jacket's made _____ very soft leather. (by / of)

4 I don't think that tie _____ with the shirt. (goes / matches)

5 This dress is too small! It just doesn't _____ . (go / fit)

6 Can I try this suit _____ , please? (out / on)

7 He's _____ a very old raincoat. (putting / wearing)

8 One of the _____ is missing from this blouse. (belts / buttons)

OVER TO YOU

What kind of clothes do you think are fashionable at the moment?

What type of clothes do you like wearing?

Recycling

A Which countries are these towns or cities in?

1 Berne	6 Buenos Aires	11 Reykjavik	16 Melbourne
2 Delphi	7 Amsterdam	12 Beijing	17 Rio de Janeiro
3 Toulouse	8 Bonn	13 Glasgow	18 Salzburg
4 Ankara	9 Cardiff	14 Valletta	19 Seoul
5 Milan	10 Oporto	15 Toledo	20 Mumbai

B Look at the course dates and answer the questions.

Weekend Courses at the Howarth Community Centre in 2005 and 2006

Computer Studies 18–20/2/05
Car Maintenance 11–13/3/05
Advanced Spoken French 27–29/5/05
Japanese for Beginners 8–10/7/05
Flower Arranging 2–4/9/05

Start Your Own Business 18–20/11/05
Yoga 22–24/1/06
Writing Poetry 2–4/4/06
Oriental Cooking 7–9/5/06

In which month can you ...
1 practise a language you already know?
2 learn a relaxing type of exercise?
3 prepare for your new job in Tokyo?
4 learn about word processing and software?
5 find out how to look after your car?
6 learn how to make your home look more attractive?
7 discover how to change your career?

C Which is the odd one out in these groups of words, and why?

1 sandals   trainers   slippers   gloves   boots
2 jeans   trousers   dress   tights   socks   shorts
3 striped   swimsuit   patterned   plain   checked
4 hat   coat   sandals   scarf   gloves
5 waistcoat   leather   wool   silk   cotton   polyester

D Some of these sentences are not correct. Tick (✔) the right ones, and correct the wrong ones.

1 You use a washing machine to wash your dirty dishes.
2 The fridge is the best place to keep ice cream and frozen food for a long time.
3 Dinner plates are usually stored in wardrobes when they are not being used.
4 You can pile up pots and pans in the sink, and wash them later.
5 A chest of drawers is very useful for hanging your clothes.

Units and containers

a bag of flour, sugar, potatoes	**a bottle** of oil, water, wine, shampoo	**a kilo / pound** of carrots
a packet of biscuits, butter, sweets, cereal, tea bags	**a can** of coke, lemonade	**a litre / pint** of milk
a box of chocolates, matches	**a carton** of fruit juice, milk, yogurt	**a loaf** / two **loaves** of bread
a bar of soap, chocolate	**a jug** of milk	**a slice / piece** of cake, meat, bread, toast, cheese
a tube of toothpaste, glue, tomato puree	**a cup / pot** of tea, coffee	**a plate** of food
a tin of tomatoes, soup, fruit	**a glass** of water, milk, juice	**a bowl** of soup, cereal
		a dish of vegetables
		a jar / pot of jam, honey

A Complete the sentences with words from the study box.

1 Can you open this _____ of juice for me? I just can't do it!

2 She always has a _____ of biscuits with her, in case she gets hungry in meetings!

3 You can get the meat ready for the barbecue, while I look for the matches. I'm sure we've got a _____ somewhere.

4 All the children who ran the race received a small prize – a _____ of sweets.

5 The boy finished drinking his coke, and carefully put the _____ in the litter bin.

6 Mrs Rigg picked a lot of strawberries last summer, and made fifteen _____ of jam.

7 I'm not buying any more toothpaste yet. There's still plenty left in that _____ !

8 Could you possibly go to the corner shop and buy me a _____ of butter? I've completely run out.

B Complete the shopping list with words from the study box.

1 large _____ of cereal		1 _____ of butter	
1 _____ of chocolate		2 small _____ of brown bread	
2 _____ of white sugar		a _____ of cheese	
1 _____ of chicken soup		1 _____ of glue	
1 _____ of shampoo		1 _____ of flour	
2 _____ of milk		1 _____ of honey	

OVER TO YOU

What do you usually have for breakfast or lunch?

Sports and hobbies

free / spare / leisure time	play / win / lose a game / match	badminton / squash / tennis **racket**	badminton / squash / tennis / basketball / volleyball **court**
join a class / club	beat the other team / side	baseball / cricket / table tennis **bat**	cricket / football / hockey **pitch**
do judo / karate / yoga / aerobics	player	golf **club**	swimming **pool**
go to the gym	referee	fishing **rod**	skating **rink**
go cycling / skiing / hiking / jogging	supporter / fan	snowboarding	golf **course**
play a sport	score a goal	skateboarding	
take up / give up a sport		(rock) climbing	*He's good at tennis.*
play **the** guitar/ piano	*What's the score?*	canoeing	
	It's two-nil.	stamp collecting	
	It's a draw.		

A Match the words A–E with the sports. Use each item only once.

1 baseball   A court
2 swimming   B rod
3 tennis   C bat
4 football   D pool
5 fishing   E pitch

B Matt and Tom support their local football team, but Matt couldn't go to watch them play last week. Complete the conversation with words from the study box.

Matt: How was the 1) _____ last week?

Tom: It was brilliant! We 2) _____ the other side, of course!

Matt: Great! How many goals did we 3) _____ ?

Tom: Two. Well, three, really, but the 4) _____ didn't allow the last one.

Matt: How many more 5) _____ are there this season?

Tom: Only four more. If we 6) _____ them all, we've got a chance of winning the Cup!

Matt: I think we can do it. We've got such good 7) _____ in the team now, we really can't 8) _____ !

C Choose the correct word from the pair in brackets to complete the sentences.

1 In my _____ time I go to evening classes to study architecture. (spare / extra)

2 My brother's main hobby is _____ old postcards. (gathering / collecting)

3 Can I borrow your _____ ? Kurt's just invited me to play a game of tennis. (bat / racket)

4 My brother is joining the cricket team, so he'll have to buy a new _____ . (club / bat)

5 The doctors told my uncle to _____ up squash, because it was too energetic for him. (take / give)

OVER TO YOU   What are your interests, sports and other hobbies?

Work and jobs

employer	factory	doctor	computer programmer
employee	office	dentist	electrician
boss	studio	nurse	engineer
colleague	garage	teacher	plumber
staff	school	lawyer	mechanic
	surgery	policeman / woman	fireman / firefighter
apply for a job	hospital	vet	shop assistant
resign	lab(oratory)	architect	factory worker
retire	department store	manager	taxi driver
	supermarket	secretary	actor / actress
	call centre	journalist	artist

What do you do? (= What's your job?)   *I'm a student.*   *He works with computers.*

A Find the correct job title from the study box to fit the job description.

1 Someone who paints pictures or does other creative work.
2 Someone who is in charge of an office, factory or company.
3 Someone who repairs water or heating systems.
4 Someone who designs or draws plans for new buildings.
5 Someone who looks after animals if they are ill.
6 Someone who writes articles for a newspaper.
7 Someone who can invent or design new machinery.
8 Someone who works as part of a team putting together or preparing things which the company will sell.

B Match the places of work with the jobs. Use each item only once.

1 office   A doctor
2 surgery   B artist
3 department store   C secretary
4 school   D mechanic
5 studio   E shop assistant
6 garage   F teacher

C Who would you ring up for help in the following situations? You have to take action fast!

1 The police have just arrested you for bank robbery.
2 Your TV set has just exploded with a loud bang, and all the lights are off in your house.
3 Your little brother has woken up in the middle of the night with a terrible pain in his stomach.
4 There is water all over the kitchen floor. It's still pouring out of the washing machine.
5 You have to catch a train for an important meeting, and it's too far to walk to the station.

OVER TO YOU

What kind of job do you do / would you like to do?

Travel and holidays

save up for a holiday	ticket	hotel	passport
book a flight	charter flight	guesthouse	guidebook
pack your bags	scheduled flight	(self-catering) apartment	camera
go on holiday	package holiday	villa	sunglasses
set off on a journey	travel insurance	chalet	sun cream
check in at the airport / hotel	suitcase	campsite	shorts
travel by plane / coach / train	luggage	tent	sleeping bag
stay in a hotel	currency	caravan	rucksack
have a wonderful time	credit card	youth hostel	walking boots

A Match the people with the most suitable places for them to stay on holiday. Use each item only once.

1 long-distance walkers

2 a group of friends on a skiing holiday

3 a young family with several children

4 a businessman whose expenses are paid by his company

5 students on a camping holiday

A a chalet in the Alps

B a city hotel

C a youth hostel in the countryside

D tents on a campsite

E a self-catering apartment near the beach

B You are just about to go on holiday to California, and your friend Amanda is giving you some advice. She thinks she's an expert on travelling! Complete the sentences with words from the study box.

1 Don't forget to take your new digital _____ , will you!

2 Have you got your American _____ yet? How many dollars to the pound is it at the moment?

3 If you're sunbathing, you'll have to get a powerful _____ for your fair skin! Factor 20, at least.

4 Have you remembered to arrange _____ ? You might have an accident, or need an operation, or lose all your luggage, or something!

5 I think you should take your _____ just in case. It's accepted in restaurants and hotels all over the States, and you never know, you might spend all your cash.

6 And don't forget your _____ , will you? They won't let you into the country without it!

C Complete the text with words from the study box.

Last year Amanda saved 1) _____ a lot of money and 2) _____ on holiday to Australia. She 3) _____ her flight and bought a really good 4) _____ on Australia. She always travels light, so she just 5) _____ a small bag, and 6) _____ off on her journey. She 7) _____ in a hotel in Sydney, and with friends in Melbourne, travelling long distances 8) _____ plane. She had a wonderful 9) _____ , and now she's an expert on Australia!

OVER TO YOU

What kind of place do you prefer staying in when you are on holiday?

Recycling

A Match the units or containers with the items A–H. Use each item only once.

1	jar	A	soap
2	loaf	B	mushroom soup
3	carton	C	water
4	bar	D	honey
5	tin	E	toothpaste
6	box	F	pure orange juice
7	bottle	G	milk chocolates
8	tube	H	brown bread

B Choose the correct word(s) from the pair in brackets to complete the sentences.

1 We'll have to stay in a _____ because we can't afford anything expensive. Luckily, we're members.   (youth hostel / hotel)

2 I'm hoping to book a _____ flight because then I know the times are fixed. And you get better service. It costs more, of course. (charter / scheduled)

3 Chris is going to pack a few things in a _____ and carry it on his back all round south-east Asia. I hope he can manage it! (luggage / rucksack)

4 We're going to share a _____ near the beach with some friends. It's got a swimming pool!   (tent / villa)

5 Ted bought a _____ , for information on where to stay and what places to visit.   (map / guidebook)

C Read the text and choose the correct word (A, B, C or D) for each space.

Tony Milligan started his working life as a factory worker in a small 1) _____ , and, by working hard, he became the 2) _____ after a few years. The company continued to do well, mostly because Tony believed in good conditions for his 3) _____ . There was a friendly atmosphere, and people enjoyed their work. When someone reached 60 or 65 and 4) _____ , Tony always gave a party for them, and a generous present. At break times there was always a fresh 5) _____ of tea or coffee ready for the workers, and if anyone fell ill, Tony sent him or her straight to the doctor's 6) _____ by taxi. Local people knew what a good 7) _____ he was, and whenever there was a 8) _____ available at Tony's factory, a lot of people 9) _____ for it.

	A	B	C	D
1	office	factory	studio	room
2	manager	employee	engineer	mechanic
3	assistants	employers	boss	staff
4	resigned	applied	retired	retreated
5	glass	pot	carton	box
6	hospital	studio	clinic	surgery
7	boss	chief	patron	staff
8	work	employ	job	profession
9	resigned	applied	retired	demanded

Scenery

north	mountain	lake	in the mountains / hills
south	hill	river	in / through the valleys
east	volcano	(river)bank	by the river / sea
west	cliff	stream	on the coast
	valley	canal	on the beach
city	field	bridge	
town	wood(s)	sea	flat
village	(rain)forest	ocean	hilly
farm	jungle	coast	mountainous
cottage	desert	beach	agricultural

What did you think of the scenery / countryside / landscape?
It was breathtaking / impressive / beautiful / unspoilt / nothing special.

A Some of these sentences are not correct. Tick (✔) the right ones, and correct the wrong ones.

1 A village is a large and important group of houses, shops, schools, cinemas, etc.

2 It is completely safe to live close to a volcano.

3 The needle on a compass points north, to help you find your way.

4 If you go mountain climbing, you don't need any special equipment.

5 'Did you like the scenery?' 'I'm afraid not. It was breathtaking.'

B Choose the correct word from the pair in brackets to complete the sentences.

1 There are a number of _____ in Germany, designed to carry goods from one end of the country to another.   (rivers / canals)

2 As we looked down from the plane, we could see lots of tiny _____ , like a white circle around the flat blue _____ .
(villages / towns, sea / lake)

3 There are still over 450 million hectares of Canadian _____ left. (woods / forest)

4 The helicopter had to land right on top of the snow-covered _____ to rescue the boys.   (hill / mountain)

5 Looking out of the train windows, we saw fields all the way. The scenery was very _____ .   (farming / agricultural)

6 We sunbathed on the _____ all afternoon.   (desert / beach)

C Complete the text with words from the study box.

The Alps are a natural boundary between France and Italy. If you want to climb 1) _____ , ski on the steep slopes, travel by train or by car through the narrow 2) _____ , or take boat trips on the calm 3) _____ , this is the place to do all these things. Grenoble, an old 4) _____ impressively situated on the 5) _____ of the Drac and Isère rivers, has plenty of nightlife, while from Annecy you can walk or cycle around its beautiful blue 6) _____ .

OVER TO YOU

How can you describe the scenery in your country?

What about the last place you went to on holiday? What was the scenery like there?

Entertainment

Cinema	Television	Books	Music	Theatre
trailer	soap opera	novel	opera	play
horror film	documentary	thriller	classical music	musical
romantic film	chat show	love story	pop	comedy
action movie	quiz show	detective story	jazz	tragedy
western	cartoon	ghost story	rock	ballet
special effects	commercial	science fiction	folk	
		biography		

What kind of music do you like?   Pop and rock are my favourites.

A Read the following, and decide exactly what type of book, film, music, theatre or television programme they come from. Use words from the study box to answer.

1 'Darling, I'll always love you!' (book) _____

2 'So tell me, Wayne, what happened when your first record reached number one?' (television) _____

3 'Coming to a cinema near you, very soon ...' (cinema) _____

4 'If you leave me, I'll have nothing! My life is worth nothing without you! Stay with me!' (*Door bangs. Sound of crying*) (theatre) _____

5 Baby baby you're my love Baby baby stars above Ooh baby don't you know Baby baby love you so ... (music) _____

6 'Now, your question for two points. What's the capital of the Czech Republic?' (television) _____

7 The door opened slowly, and out of the darkness came a thin white hand. There was a strange moaning sound and ... (book) _____

8 'Oh, no, how am I ever going to get his shirt clean?' 'Don't worry, Whizz is here! Whizz will solve your problem, like magic!' (television) _____

9 'OK, you guys, drop those guns and let the old man go!' (film) _____

B Read the sentences and complete the words.

1 Spielberg's films are well known for their s _____ e _____ .

2 *Tom and Jerry* is one of the best American c _____ ever made.

3 There was an excellent d _____ on the country's tax problems on television last night.

4 Catherine always watches her favourite q _____ s _____ , just to see if she can get the answers right!

5 Rudolf Nureyev and Margot Fonteyn were perhaps the world's most famous pair of b _____ dancers.

6 Stories about what could happen in the future are called s_____ f_____ .

7 *A* I went to see a Shakespeare play yesterday.

   B Was it a c _____ or a tragedy?

OVER TO YOU   What are your favourite kinds of entertainment?

Health and the body

spots	flu	head	arm	leg
a rash	a cold	ear	elbow	knee
a cut	a cough	mouth	wrist	ankle
a bruise	a sore throat	nose	hand	foot
a black eye	a headache	cheek	fingers	toes
medicine	(a) stomachache	neck	thumb	stomach
an injection	(an) earache	back	waist	chest
	a broken bone	shoulder	hip	heart

I've got a pain in my back.   My back hurts.   I've got backache.

A Match what the doctor says with the illnesses or problems. Use each item only once.

1 Take two aspirin and lie down.
2 Go to the hospital and they'll put it in plaster.
3 There's no medicine for it, but try taking extra vitamin C.
4 You don't smoke, do you?
5 Go straight to bed, drink lots of liquid and don't get up till you feel better.
6 Put this cream on, night and morning.

A a broken arm
B a cold
C flu
D a headache
E a rash
F a cough

B Label this drawing of the human body with words from the study box.

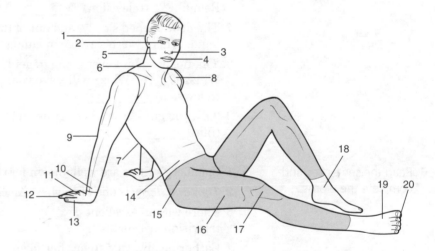

C Underline the correct alternative in the phrases.

1 break a *leg / waist*
2 open your *elbow / mouth*
3 twist an *ankle / eye*
4 count your *hips / toes*
5 bend your *knee / stomach*
6 shake *ears / hands* with someone
7 press down with a *thumb / neck*
8 relax your *heart / shoulders*
9 put a *cheek / foot* in plaster
10 blow your *mouth / nose*

OVER TO YOU

Describe how you are feeling today.

Describe what was wrong with you last time you were ill.

UNIT 49

Animals

Pets	Places to keep pets	Wild animals / birds		Domestic animals	
dog	kennel	lion	fox	cow	donkey
cat	basket	tiger	rabbit	calf	goat
horse	stable	elephant	bear	bull	hen
hamster	cage	rhinoceros	mouse	sheep	chicken
fish	tank	giraffe	snake	lamb	duck
goldfish	bowl	monkey	crocodile	pig	turkey
		parrot	whale	sheepdog	camel
		penguin	dolphin		

A Find the correct animal from the study box to fit the description.

1 It's like a large cat, and is a dangerous animal, sometimes called the king of the jungle.

2 It's a very large, heavy animal, with a horn growing on its head.

3 It's the largest warm-blooded animal, and lives in the sea.

4 It's very large and heavy, with big ears and a long nose called a trunk.

5 It's a very small pet. It looks like a fat mouse, and moves around fast.

6 It's another large cat, with stripes all over its body.

B Match the animals with the places where they live. Use each item only once.

1	dog	A	cage
2	sheep	B	stable
3	crocodile	C	hole
4	whale	D	jungle
5	hamster	E	kennel
6	monkey	F	ocean
7	horse	G	farm
8	mouse	H	river

C Complete the text with words from the study box.

Joseph wanted to have an animal of his own. So one day he asked his parents, 'Do you think I could have a 1) _____ ?'

'What kind of pet?' asked his mother. 'You haven't got time to take a 2) _____ for a walk every day, you know.'

'And we aren't going to buy you a 3) _____ !' said his father. 'Riding lessons are much too expensive.'

'Could I have a 4) _____ ?' asked Joseph. 'We've got an old basket for it to sleep in. It would just eat a bit of fish, and drink milk.'

'No, I don't like them,' said his mother. 'They catch birds. How about a 5) _____ ? It's a small animal, and we can buy a cage for it to live in.'

'Oh yes!' said Joseph. 'And I promise to look after it myself!'

OVER TO YOU

Do you like animals? Have you got any pets?

UNIT 50

Recycling

A Where is your ...? Match the parts of the human body with where they are (A or B).

1 cheek	A between nose and ear	B between eyes and hair
2 wrist	A between arm and shoulder	B between hand and arm
3 fingers	A on your feet	B on your hands
4 elbow	A on your leg	B on your arm

Now match the health problems with their meanings (A or B).

5 a rash	A lots of spots	B feeling very tired
6 flu	A feeling hot and cold, and ill	B coughing all the time
7 toothache	A you need to brush your teeth	B your tooth hurts
8 a broken ankle	A you can't walk	B you can't write

B Put these words into pairs that have something in common, and find the word or phrase in capitals that connects them.
EXAMPLE:
sea, ocean, SALT

1 north	A field	HOME
2 river	B mountain	WATER
3 farm	C south	TREES
4 hill	D woods	DIRECTION
5 house	E canal	SAND
6 forest	F cottage	ANIMALS
7 desert	G village	PEOPLE
8 town	H beach	A HIGH PLACE

C Decide which television programme is most suitable for these people.

1 An old lady who likes hearing about people's private lives.
2 A girl of fourteen who likes romance and love stories.
3 Children who are about five years old.
4 A businessman who enjoys serious programmes about money.

A **Vista** Cash in hand
Second of the documentary series on big business and the banks

B **Snow White**
Another chance to see the popular Walt Disney cartoon

C **Dark Stranger**
Who is the man Eva meets on the train? Will she ever see him again? A story of great passion, set in the South of France

D **Good Morning, World!**
Today Richard talks to the pop star Zap, and Jane finds out what the Princess of Kent does in her spare time.

Food and drink

Meat	Seafood	Vegetables	Fruit	Other	Cooking
beef	fish	beans	apples	biscuits	bake
chicken	cod	broccoli	apricots	bread	boil
duck	prawns	cabbage	bananas	cake	fry
lamb	salmon	carrots	cherries	chips	grill
pork	squid	cauliflower	grapefruit	pasta	poach
steak	trout	courgettes	grapes	rice	roast
turkey	tuna	cucumber	lemons	toast	steam
veal	**Dairy etc**	garlic	melon	curry	
bacon	butter	lettuce	oranges		herbs
ham	cheese	onions	peaches	coffee	spices
sausages	cream	peas	pears	fruit juice	salt
	milk	peppers	pineapple	lemonade	pepper
	yogurt	potatoes	raspberries	mineral water	oil
	eggs	tomatoes	strawberries	tea	vinegar

Opposites: delicious ~ tasteless   greasy ~ dry   overcooked ~ undercooked
hard ~ soft   hot ~ cold   sweet ~ sour   spicy / hot ~ mild   strong ~ weak

A Match the types of food with the ways they are cooked. Use each item only once.

1 roast meat   A cooked in hot oil
2 a fried tomato   B cooked in its juice or in a little oil in the oven
3 steamed cabbage   C cooked in boiling water
4 a poached egg   D cooked under the grill
5 pasta   E broken and cooked lightly in water
6 a baked potato   F cooked in the oven in its skin, with no fat or oil
7 grilled fish   G cooked over boiling water, not in it

B Which is the odd one out in these groups of words, and why?

1 lamb   cod   beef   pork   chicken
2 oranges   pineapple   lettuce   grapes   bananas
3 cucumber   courgettes   lettuce   broccoli   carrots
4 poach   steam   bake   boil
5 mineral water   tea   lemonade   fruit juice

C What would you say to the waiter in these situations?
EXAMPLE:
Your cabbage is full of water and very soft. You say, *'Excuse me, this cabbage is overcooked.'*

1 Your steak is swimming in oil.
2 Your chicken soup isn't hot enough.
3 Your meat is red inside. You wonder if it has been cooked at all!
4 The curry you are eating has burnt your mouth.
5 Your cheesecake is the best you've ever tasted.
6 Your fish has no sauce on it, and tastes like a piece of wood.

OVER TO YOU

What are your favourite types of food? Is there any food you don't like?

UNIT 52

Friends and family

friendship	adults	grandfather	grandmother
relationship	parents	father	mother
good friend	husband	brother	sister
close friend	wife	son	daughter
boy / girlfriend	child(ren)	grandson	granddaughter
fiancé(e)	relations	uncle	aunt
keep in touch (with)	father / son /	nephew	niece
fall in love (with)	brother-in-law	stepfather	stepmother
go out with	mother / daughter /		
get engaged (to)	sister-in-law		
get married (to) / marry	cousin		

A Match the words 1–10 with their meanings A–J. Use each item only once.

1 brother-in-law   A your sister's / brother's son

2 aunt   B your father's / mother's brother

3 stepmother   C your wife's / husband's brother

4 grandfather   D anyone's girl child

5 parents   E your uncle's / aunt's child

6 nephew   F your sister's / brother's daughter

7 daughter   G your mother's / father's sister

8 uncle   H anyone's mother and father

9 cousin   I your father's / mother's father

10 niece   J your father's second wife (not your real mother)

B Choose the correct word from the pair in brackets to complete the sentences.

1 Flora had to ask her _____ for permission to go out in the evenings. (fathers / parents)

2 Victoria and Rafael have been married for ten years now. They have a wonderful _____ . (relationship / friendship)

3 Fred gave a large present to his _____ , but she never thanked him for it. (nephew / niece)

4 Georgia and her mother lived together in their family home. When Theo married Georgia and came to live with them, he got on surprisingly well with his _____ . (stepmother / mother-in-law)

5 'How well do you know Nadia?' 'Oh, she's a _____ friend.' (near / close)

OVER TO YOU

Do you like having one or two really close friends, or lots of (not so close) friends?

How many brothers and sisters have you got? How old are they? Where do they live?

How often do you see all your family (uncles, aunts, cousins, grandparents)?

Weather

rain ~ rainy	warm	drought	**Seasons**
sun ~ sunny	hot	heatwave	spring
fog ~ foggy	*It's boiling!*	a cold / hot / wet spell	summer
mist ~ misty	cold	a fine / dry day	autumn
cloud(s) ~ cloudy	chilly	a grey / dull day	winter
shower ~ showery	*It's freezing!*	flood, floods	
frost ~ frosty	*It's snowing.*	breeze	
ice ~ icy	wet	storm	
snow ~ snowy	*It's raining.*	gale	
wind ~ windy	*It's pouring!*	hurricane	

What's the temperature today? *It's over 40 degrees.* *What's the weather like?*

A What was the weather like? Look at the descriptions and use words from the study box to complete the sentences.

1 We could only see a metre in front of us. It was very _____ .

2 The rain stopped and started all day. It was _____ .

3 It was really cold when we came out of the party. It was _____ .

4 It was raining really hard all day. It was _____ .

5 It was a bit cold so I put a pullover on. It was _____ .

6 It was terribly hot that day. It was _____ .

B Complete the sentences with words from the study box.

1 The ground is dry, and we haven't had any rain for months. It's a real _____ .

2 Ken sat in his sailing boat, just waiting for a _____ to fill the sail and start the boat moving.

3 Because it rained non-stop for six weeks, there are _____ in the area, with fields and villages under water.

4 The great _____ of 1987 blew down many trees that had stood in the park for a hundred years.

5 It's been unusually cold for some time. We don't often have a cold _____ in August. It's supposed to be summer!

C Match the words or phrases with the general descriptions A–D.

1 sun	____	8 frost	____	A WINDY	
2 rain	____	9 It's pouring!	____		
3 breeze	____	10 It's chilly.	____	B WET	
4 gale	____	11 It's boiling!	____		
5 ice	____	12 heatwave	____	C COLD	
6 snow	____	13 floods	____		
7 shower	____	14 It's freezing!	____	D WARM	

OVER TO YOU

What kind of weather do you have in your country? Is it different in different seasons and in different regions?

What is your favourite kind of weather? And your favourite season?

Education

lesson	subject	revise for	start school	education
class	study	an exam	leave school	university
teacher	timetable	take an exam	private school	college
pupil	break	pass an exam	state school	professor
desk	homework	fail an exam	primary school	lecturer
blackboard	rules	mark(s)	secondary school	course
whiteboard	uniform	(exam) results		student

A Complete the text with words from the study box.

Chantal's parents didn't have much money, so they sent her to a 1) _____ primary school when she was five. She enjoyed her reading and writing 2) _____ , but there were so many 3) _____ in the 4) _____ that the teacher found it difficult to control them.

When Chantal was eleven, her father got a better job, and decided to spend some money on her 5) _____ . He sent her to an expensive 6) _____ school, where the girls wore dark green 7) _____ and did two hours' 8) _____ every evening.

Chantal liked her new school, and did well. Because she studied hard, she 9) _____ all her exams, and went to university at eighteen. She chose a history 10) _____ and was an excellent 11) _____ . In the end she decided to become a 12) _____ , and returned to her old primary school to teach.

B Choose the correct word from the pair in brackets to complete the sentences.

1 There are several very good business studies _____ at Amir's university.   (careers / courses)

2 Elena is _____ her exam tomorrow.   (passing / taking)

3 Ursula is the _____ I have for German conversation. (professor / teacher)

4 Sally's at _____ school now that she's over eleven. (secondary / primary)

5 I think you'd better stay in tonight and _____ for your test tomorrow.   (revise / review)

6 Lydia's only six but she's the best _____ I've ever had. (pupil / student)

7 How much _____ do you have every day? (housework / homework)

8 What's the _____ at your college? Do you study all day? (timetable / programme)

OVER TO YOU

In your country ...

At what age do children start school, and leave school?

At what age do pupils / students take important exams?

What subjects do students study at sixteen?

Do you have state and private schools? Which do you think are better?

Do you have a school uniform? What do you think of it?

Recycling

A What relation is ...? Complete the sentences.

1 Erika is my father's second wife. She's my _____ .

2 Isabelle is my father's brother's daughter. She's my _____ .

3 Simon is my mother's brother. He's my _____ .

4 Sheila is my sister's daughter. She's my _____ .

5 Kallitsa is my husband's mother. She's my _____ .

6 Steve is my brother's son. He's my _____ .

7 Max is Sophie's husband's brother. He's Sophie's _____ .

8 Fatima is Claudia's father's sister. She's Claudia's _____ .

B Choose the correct word from the pair in brackets to complete the sentences.

1 There isn't enough _____ for skiing yet. (ice / snow)

2 It's sunny now, but it's going to _____ later. (shower / rain)

3 You'd better take an umbrella. I think there'll be _____ this afternoon. (floods / rain)

4 The old apple tree fell down in the _____ . (breeze / gale)

5 It's so _____ today. We need air conditioning! (chilly / hot)

6 We haven't had a _____ like this for years. (drought / desert)

7 It rained all day, so the roads were _____ . (pouring / wet)

8 Can you put the heating on? It's _____ ! (freezing / boiling)

C Read the text about healthy eating and choose the correct word (A, B, C, or D) for each space.

It's important to eat well, especially when you're 1) _____ . If you're at 2) _____ , you may go home for lunch, and have a cooked meal of 3) _____ or fish and vegetables. Or perhaps you take some food with you to school, and eat it in the lunch 4) _____ . A chicken and lettuce sandwich, with some fresh 5) _____ , would be a light but healthy lunch. Many people around the world eat plain, 6) _____ rice two or three times a day.

Pupils and 7) _____ often don't eat well when they're 8) _____ for an exam — they eat chocolate and drink lots of black coffee! And by the way, doctors say everybody should start the day with a healthy 9) _____ . It's also good for you to drink a lot of 10) _____ right through the day.

	A	B	C	D
1	student	study	studying	studied
2	school	primary	office	class
3	cheese	meat	fruit	seafood
4	timetable	classroom	lesson	break
5	lemons	fruit	chicken	peas
6	boiled	baked	grilled	roast
7	teachers	professors	students	boys
8	reviewing	reading	learning	revising
9	dinner	breakfast	lunch	supper
10	water	coffee	tea	coke

Hello and goodbye

Meeting for the first time
A Hello, nice / pleased to meet you.   B Nice / pleased to meet you.
A How do you do?   B How do you do?
A Hello, what's your name?   B I'm Clare. What's yours?

Meeting people again
A Hello, how are you?   B Fine, thanks, and you?
A Hello, there!   B Hi! Haven't seen you for ages!
A Fancy seeing you again!   B Yes, nice to see you again!
A Sorry, do I know you?   B We've met before, haven't we?

David, have you met my brother?   David, this is Frank.

Saying goodbye
Well, goodbye then.   It was nice meeting you.   I'll be in touch.
Goodbye.   We must keep in touch.   We must get together sometime.
Bye.   See you later.   See you soon.   All the best.

A Match the two parts of the short conversations. Use each item only once.

1 How do you do?
2 How are you?
3 Hello, what's your name?
4 Pleased to meet you.
5 We must keep in touch.
6 Sorry, do I know you?

A Pleased to meet *you*.
B Yes, we must.
C Fine, thanks, and you?
D I think we've met before.
E How do you do?
F I'm Richard. What's yours?

B Look at the situations and respond, using expressions from the study box.

1 You meet a business colleague, a manager from another company, for the first time.

2 You meet a friend of your sister's for the first time.

3 Your sister didn't tell you her friend's name.

4 She says her name is Jill. You meet her again, in town, later the same day.

5 You're with your cousin Maurice. You want Jill to meet Maurice.

6 Someone at a party calls your name. You don't recognise or remember this person at all.

7 Your friend introduces you to someone new. You think perhaps you know him or her already, but you're not sure.

8 You are the first to leave a business meeting. You want to say that you will speak to, phone or e-mail the others soon.

9 You're saying goodbye to some friends in the street. You expect to see them later that evening.

10 You're saying goodbye to a friend on the phone. You aren't sure when you'll see him or her again.

Talking about yourself

My name's Stuart.   I live at 24 Arden Road.   I come from Scotland.
I'm single. I'm engaged.   I live in Edinburgh.   I'm from Scotland.
I'm married. I'm divorced.   I live in Scotland.   I'm Scottish.

I live in a flat / house / bungalow / caravan.   I speak French / Greek / Arabic.
I'm a student / teacher / doctor / secretary.   I'm studying maths / music / science.
I'm an artist / architect / engineer.   I'm unemployed.   I work in a studio / factory / an office.

My hobbies are reading / travelling / playing football.
In my spare time I like watching films / going to the theatre / playing the guitar.

A Complete the text with words from the study box.

Here is some information about our new secretary. Her 1) _____ is Denise and she comes 2) _____ Switzerland. She 3) _____ French, German and English. She's been 4) _____ secretary for the last five years, since she finished her training, although for six months she didn't have a job and was 5) _____ . She lives 6) _____ a flat, 7) _____ 103A Salisbury Street, and she's 8) _____ . But she's getting married next summer. Her 9) _____ are going to 10) _____ cinema, playing 11) _____ piano, and 12) _____ to faraway places. I'm sure you'll all like her!

B Choose the correct word(s) from the pair in brackets to complete the sentences.

1 Alan hasn't much money, and doesn't like staying in one place, so he lives in a _____ , which he can move around the country. (bungalow / caravan)

2 Celia's marriage broke up, so now she's _____ . (engaged / divorced)

3 Rosemary is _____ Ireland.   (coming from / from)

4 Douglas _____ Japanese very well.   (talks / speaks)

5 Helen is _____ excellent car mechanic.   (a / an)

6 Hassan's main hobby is _____ his football team. (support / supporting)

7 Andrew lives _____ Istanbul these days.   (in / at)

8 There are at least fifty _____ people in Elisa's village. (unemployed / workless)

C Talk and write about yourself, using expressions from the study box.

We want to know:

… your name and where you live

… where you come from and your nationality

… if you're a student or have a job

… if you're single or not

… what languages you speak

… what subjects you study

… what your hobbies are.

Keeping conversation going

Really? How interesting! How fascinating! How lovely! Oh dear!
*How sad! I see. What do **you** think, Silvia? Going back to what you were saying …*
What did you do next?

The listener can use **short questions** to encourage the speaker or to show interest:

A He speaks Arabic. B Does he?   A He went there yesterday. B Did he?

A I'm very unhappy. B Are you?   A I'm not staying. B Aren't you?

A We've done it! B Have we?   A I won't see him. B Won't you?

Note: *A **He's** been there before. B **Has** he?   A **He's** Colombian. B **Is** he?*

The speaker can use question tags to make sure the listener is really listening:

Anne looks tired, doesn't she?   You didn't see him, did you?

It's raining now, isn't it?   You're French, aren't you?

Note: *He's arrived, **hasn't** he?   He's wonderful, **isn't** he?*

A Complete the listener's comments, showing interest.

1 *A* They bought some presents.   *B* Oh, _____ they?
2 *A* She plays tennis very well.   *B* Oh, _____ she?
3 *A* I was waiting for you.   *B* Oh, _____ you?
4 *A* I've finished the book.   *B* Oh, _____ you?
5 *A* I didn't have any lunch yesterday.   *B* Oh, _____ you?

B Complete the speaker's question tags, to keep conversation going.

1 He won't be here on Tuesday, _____ he?
2 She's paid for it, _____ she?
3 She could be here by now, _____ she?
4 He's intelligent, _____ he?
5 They didn't tell the truth, _____ they?
6 You can't swim, _____ you?
7 It isn't snowing, _____ it?
8 She speaks Greek, _____ she?
9 You love her, _____ you?
10 You're Welsh, _____ you?

C Make questions to keep conversation going, using the words given.

1 So where exactly / you / live?
2 How many brothers / sisters / you / got?
3 How / you / come / school / work?
4 How long / it / take?
5 Where / you / have / lunch?
6 What / you / have / breakfast / lunch / dinner?
7 What / your hobbies?
8 Where / you / go / holidays every year?
9 What kind / music / films / books / you / like best?
10 What subjects / you / like / study / talk about / write about?

Checking meaning

> **If you didn't hear:** *Pardon?   Sorry?   What was that?   What did you say?*
> *Sorry, could you repeat that?   I didn't quite catch that.   I didn't hear what you said.*
>
> **If you didn't understand:** *What do you mean?   I don't (quite / really) understand.*
> *What's the point of that?   Can you explain what you mean?*
>
> **If you aren't sure:** *Do you mean ...?   I'm not sure I quite understand.*
> *What do you mean exactly?   I'm not sure what ... means.   I don't follow.*
>
> **If you want to check:** *So what you're saying is ...   You're saying you want ...*
> *Right, I'll ..., shall I?   So the way to do it is ...   You mean, you think ...*

A Look at the signs. You are not sure what they mean. Ask a friend about them, using language from the study box.

EXAMPLE:

NO SMOKING

Does this mean we mustn't smoke in this room, or in the whole building?

1 VOUCHER PARKING ONLY

2 FOR USE OF MEMBERS ONLY

3 DO NOT DISTURB

4 NO CHILDREN BEYOND THIS POINT

5 UP TO TWELVE ITEMS ONLY

6 DOGS MUST BE HELD

B Look at the situations and respond, using expressions from the study box.

1 A friend is talking to you on the phone. You can't hear him well. He says, 'And then we went to the Pegarama,' or something like that.

2 Your uncle, who used to be an explorer in Africa, is explaining to you what to do if a large animal like a rhino or an elephant attacks you. He says, 'Rhinos usually only run in a straight line. So it's a good idea to zigzag when you run away.' You aren't sure what he means.

3 A nurse is telling your class about first aid, so that you know what to do if someone is ill or hurt. She says, 'And if someone's got something in their mouth or throat, so they can't breathe, use the Heimlich manoeuvre.' You have no idea what this is.

4 Your brother is explaining the rules of hockey to you. He says, 'If the teams have the same score at the end, we need extra time or sudden death.' You've never heard of 'sudden death'.

5 Someone is pointing out the stars in the sky. He says, 'The Milky Way passes by the feet of the Twins, Castor and Pollux.' You aren't sure of these names, or what he means.

6 Your boss is giving you instructions for next week, when he'll be away, and you'll have the keys to the office. He says, 'Now remember, switch off the photocopier, switch on the answerphone, and set the security alarm before you leave every night.' You want to check that you understand.

7 A friend is talking about her ideas for improving life in your town. She says, 'Everything's so small here! We need bigger schools, bigger hospitals!' You don't understand why. Ask her to explain her opinions.

Finding your way and giving directions

Excuse me, can / could you tell me the way to the police station, please?
Excuse me, how do I get to the hospital?
Excuse me, is this the way to the railway station?
Excuse me, where's the nearest chemist, please?
Is there somewhere near here that sells newspapers?
Is there a bank near here?
Where's the best place to park round here?

Go up / down / along Station Road and turn right at the traffic lights.
Go straight ahead / on until you reach the roundabout, and take the second exit.
Go over the crossroads / bridge, carry on past the school, and then ask again.
It's / Take the first turning (on the) right, just past the library.

It's on the corner of Queen's Road and King Street. You'll see a yellow sign.
Let me think / see – yes, it's just up here on the left, opposite the museum.
I'm sorry, I have no idea. I'm a stranger here myself!
It's only another fifty metres. It's not far. It's a bit further on. You can't miss it.

A Look at the map.
Choose different places
to start from and ask for
directions to:
1 the nearest chemist
2 the theatre
3 the health centre
4 the library
5 the supermarket
6 the nearest bank

Answer the questions by
giving directions. Practise
in pairs if you can.

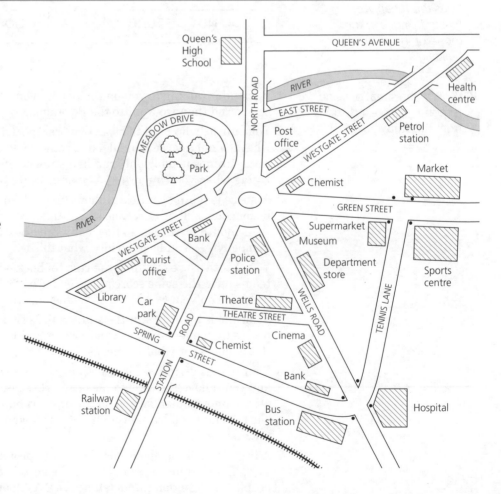

B Complete the three conversations about finding the way, using words from the study box. Put **one** word in each space.

1 A 1)_____ me, could you tell me the 2) _____ to the park?
 B Let me 3)_____ . Yes, go 4)_____ on and take the first 5)_____ on the left.
 A Is it 6)_____ ?
 B No, only about 100 metres. You can't 7)_____ it.
 A Thanks a lot.

2 A Excuse me, is 1)_____ the way to the railway 2)_____ ?
 B I'm sorry, I have no 3)_____ . I'm a 4)_____ here myself!
 A Thanks anyway.

3 A Excuse me, is there 1)_____ near here that sells maps?
 B You could try the bookshop. It's a bit 2)_____ on, next to the post office. It's on the 3)_____ of East Street.
 A Thank you very much.

C Find the unnecessary word in each sentence and circle it.

1 You'll find the museum on the left side.
2 Go straight along the Smith Street.
3 Me, I'm a stranger here myself!
4 Could you tell me the suitable way to the gym?
5 I think it's left opposite the primary school.
6 Is there a department store near to here?

D Underline the correct words to complete the sentences.

1 Excuse me, how do I *get / go* to the theatre from here?
2 Is this the *road / way* to the market?
3 Could you *say / tell* me the way to the college, please?
4 Excuse me, where's the *nearest / next* petrol station?
5 Go on down Market Street *passed / past* the department store.
6 It's straight ahead until you *come / reach* the crossroads.
7 Go *along / on* Green Lane and it's on your left.
8 At the end of the street, *take / turn* right.
9 It's a bit *further / way* on, on the right.

E Answer the questions, using expressions from the study box.

From the bus or railway station in your town, how do you get to
a) your home?
b) the hospital?
c) the shopping centre?

From your home, how do you get to
a) the nearest airport?
b) the nearest supermarket?
c) the nearest sports centre?

Understanding signs and notices

A Match these words from signs and notices with their meanings.

1	required	A	proof of age and identity
2	permitted	B	reduction, lower price
3	public access	C	rubbish (e.g. empty packets, old papers)
4	ID	D	wait in a line
5	in progress	E	people with a physical problem
6	queue	F	thieves who steal from people's bags or pockets
7	discount	G	the right for anybody to enter
8	the disabled	H	going on at the moment
9	pickpockets	I	be careful
10	beware	J	allowed
11	footpath	K	needed
12	litter	L	walking route

B Where are you most likely to see these notices? Choose the best answer.

1
| **10% STUDENT DISCOUNT** |

a) in a school
b) in a shop
c) in an office

2
| **DISABLED PARKING ONLY** |

a) outside a supermarket
b) on a footpath
c) 100 metres from a hospital

3
| **FISHING BY PERMIT ONLY** |

a) in a fish market
b) beside a river
c) on the beach

4
| **NO UNDER-18s – ID REQUIRED** |

a) at a theatre
b) at a restaurant
c) at a disco

5
| **NO RUNNING OR JUMPING** |

a) at a swimming pool
b) at a football stadium
c) at an ice rink

6
| **KEEP OFF THE GRASS** |

a) in the forest
b) on a school playing field
c) in a town park

C Match each explanation with the correct notice.

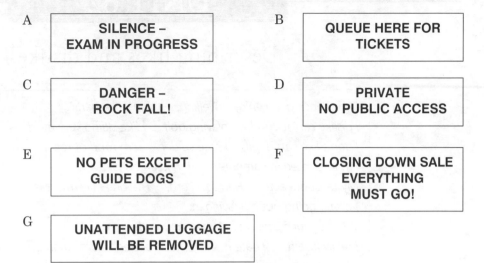

A SILENCE –
EXAM IN PROGRESS

B QUEUE HERE FOR
TICKETS

C DANGER –
ROCK FALL!

D PRIVATE
NO PUBLIC ACCESS

E NO PETS EXCEPT
GUIDE DOGS

F CLOSING DOWN SALE
EVERYTHING
MUST GO!

G UNATTENDED LUGGAGE
WILL BE REMOVED

1 Take care because the road may be blocked.

2 Animals are not allowed, apart from dogs which are used by blind people.

3 Only the owners can enter this area.

4 This shop is going out of business and selling all its goods very cheaply.

5 Wait in line, until it's your turn.

6 If you leave your bags here, they'll be taken away.

7 Be quiet because students are taking a test in a room near here.

D Look at the notices. Are the explanations true (T) or false (F)? Write **T** or **F** after each explanation, and say where you might see each sign.

1 SLOW –
ROAD WORKS

2 PICKPOCKETS OPERATING
IN THIS AREA

3 FOOTPATH ONLY

4 LADIES   GENTLEMEN

5 THREE FOR THE
PRICE OF TWO!

6 TAKE YOUR LITTER HOME
WITH YOU

7 NO SMOKING
SECTION

8 PASSPORT CONTROL

1 Work on the road is proceeding very slowly.

2 Be careful because there are thieves at work here.

3 You can ride a horse or a motorbike along here.

4 There are some important men and women here.

5 Pay for three things and receive two.

6 Don't leave any rubbish here.

7 You can smoke here.

8 Your nationality documents will be checked here.

Describing likes and dislikes

> *I like dancing.   I enjoy travelling.   I don't like garlic.*
>
> *I dislike carrots.   I love playing golf.   I like skiing very much.*
>
> *I don't like cats at all.   I hate spiders.   I'm fond of reading novels.*
>
> *I'm interested in computers.   I'm keen on jazz.*
>
> *My favourite actor is Harrison Ford.   The one I like most is ... .*
>
> *I prefer going out to staying in.*
>
> *What's your opinion of / What do you think of ...?*
>
> *I really love it.   I hate it.   It's much better / worse than ...*
>
> *It's one of the best / worst films I've ever seen.*
>
> wonderful   fantastic   brilliant   great   awful   terrible   boring
> great fun   exciting   fascinating   no fun at all   a waste of time

A Match the two halves of the sentences. Use each item only once.

1	Lisa really loves	A	in the Olympics.
2	I prefer reading	B	on snorkelling.
3	They're very fond	C	a waste of time.
4	We're interested	D	to watching videos.
5	Rachel thinks housework is	E	of camping.
6	Mark is keen	F	playing squash.

B Complete the conversation with words from the study box.

A What did you think 1) _____ the film?

B It was really 2) _____ , wasn't it? What a great film!

A Well, actually I didn't like it very 3) _____ .

B What! I thought it was great! Mind you, I didn't like the music – it was really 4) _____ .

A Well, I thought the book was 5) _____ better.

B Really? I haven't read it. But wasn't the photography 6) _____ !

A Well, yes, but the story wasn't the same as in the book. Not as exciting. In fact, I thought the film was quite 7) _____ . I nearly fell asleep!

B No! I can't believe it! It's one of the 8) _____ films I've ever seen!

C Answer the questions, using expressions from the study box.

1 What is your favourite kind of music and who is your favourite performer (singer, group, musician)?

2 What is your favourite sport, and how often do you play, or watch it? Are you a member of a team or club?

3 What do you like doing in your spare time, at evenings, weekends and on holiday? What do you dislike doing?

4 Describe a really good or bad book you have read, or a film or television programme you have seen recently. What made it so good or bad, in your opinion?

5 What do you think of ...

travelling? watching television? playing football? learning English? using a computer?

At the tourist office

A Could you help me, please?   B Certainly. I'd be glad to.
B Can I help you?   A Yes, please, I'd like some information.
A Could you tell me ... ?   B Yes, of course, ...

I'd like to find somewhere to stay / something to do round here / in the area.

Accommodation: self-catering, camping, bed and breakfast (B & B), guest house, hotel
Sightseeing: castle, palace, museum, safari park, theme park, archaeological site
Activities: hang-gliding, windsurfing, pony-trekking, guided walks
Transport: bus, coach, train, taxi, ferry, bicycle hire, car hire

timetable   leaflet   map   guidebook   footpath

Opposites: safe ~ dangerous   near ~ far away   easy ~ difficult

---

A Match the places or activities with the definitions. Use each item only once.

1 B & B	A	riding a long distance on a small horse
2 self-catering	B	sleeping outside, in a tent
3 safari park	C	flying with wings but no plane or engine
4 pony-trekking	D	place where you can drive and see wild animals
5 hotel	E	doing your own cooking
6 hang-gliding	F	place where you can see ruins of old buildings
7 archaeological site	G	guest house where you sleep and have breakfast only
8 camping	H	place to stay with good service and facilities

B Choose the correct word(s) from the pair in brackets to complete the sentences.

1 We can go hang-gliding if it doesn't _____ too much.   (cost / pay)
2 Could you give me a bus _____ , please? (programme / timetable)
3 The beach can be very _____ when the tide comes in, so please be careful.   (difficult / dangerous)
4 I can give you a free leaflet describing the walk you want, but you really need a _____ to see exactly where you're going. (map / guidebook)
5 I'm afraid the castle is too _____ for you to visit in one day. (long way / far away)
6 The village you're going to is on the other side of the river, and there's no bridge, but there *is* a _____ . (taxi / ferry)

C Imagine you are in a tourist office. Ask questions, using expressions from the study box.

1 You want to find out about places to stay in the area, places to visit, and things to do.
2 You'd like some written information, free, if possible.
3 You want to know if the beaches are safe for swimming.

At the post office and bank

Post office		Bank	
letter	registered post	cheque	account
postcard	weigh (on the scales)	credit card	statement
parcel	abroad	debit card	sign a cheque
stamp	airmail sticker	currency	cash a cheque
1st / 2nd class	customs form	change money	every month

A Complete the conversation, using expressions from the study box.

A Good morning. Could I have a 1) _____ for a letter to London, please? I want it to get there quickly.

B 2) _____ class, then. It should arrive tomorrow.

A Oh, good. And I've got a big 3) _____ to send to my brother in Scotland.

B Right, we'll have to 4) _____ it. Let's see, that's over 500 grams.

A It's a present. It cost quite a lot of money.

B Did it? Well, you could send it 5) _____ . Then, if it's lost, the Post Office will pay you some money back.

A Yes, good idea. And I've got another parcel – this one's going to Vancouver.

B Right, you'll need to fill in a 6) _____ for that one.

B Answer the questions.

1 Why do people use the 1st class post in Britain?

2 Why do people use registered post?

3 Why do you have to take a parcel to the post office before posting it?

4 What might you need if you are sending a parcel abroad?

C Match the statements and questions 1–6 with the responses A–F. Use each item only once.

1 I'd like to change some money.

2 Could I cash this cheque?

3 I'd like to pay some bills.

4 I'd like a statement.

5 Could you sign here, please?

6 How would you like it?

A Are you going to pay by cheque or card?

B Five tens, please.

C Which currency?

D You haven't signed it.

E What's your account number?

F Where? Just here? OK.

D Imagine you are at a post office or a bank. Answer the questions, using expressions from the study box.

1 Where is it going?

2 Do you want it to go 1st or 2nd class?

3 Have you recently opened an account with us?

4 How often do you want a statement?

At the restaurant and hotel

Restaurant	**Hotel**
waiter waitress menu wine list	manager receptionist porter chambermaid
to order a meal / an aperitif	*Could I book a room for tonight?*
A table for four, please.	a single / double room
Can I see the menu, please?	an en suite room / a room with private bathroom
starter: soup, fruit juice, salad, seafood	with a view of the sea / mountains
main course: meat, fish, pasta, vegetables	bed and breakfast
dessert: fruit, apple pie, ice cream	half board full board
bill tip	check in check out settle up / pay the bill
Is service included?	make / confirm a reservation
Do you accept credit cards?	

A Complete the conversation at a restaurant with words from the study box.

Man: Good evening. Can we see the 1) _____ , please?

Waiter: Yes, sir. Would you like an 2) _____ before ordering your 3) _____ ?

Man: No, thank you. Now, what shall we have as a 4) _____ ?

Woman: I think I'll have a bowl of 5) _____ to start with.

Man: And I'll have the prawn cocktail. Now what about the 6) _____ course?

Woman: I'm having the roast lamb with fresh 7) _____ . What are they exactly?

Waiter: Carrots, courgettes and potatoes, madam.

Man: And I'll have the chicken. We'll order the 8) _____ later, if we haven't eaten too much by then!

Waiter: What would you like to drink with the meal? Here's the 9) _____ list.

Man: No need, thanks. Just mineral water for both of us.

B Someone is phoning a hotel. Complete the conversation with words from the study box.

Customer: Could I 1) _____ a room for Sunday night, please?

Receptionist: A 2) _____ or a single, madam?

Customer: A double please, with 3) _____ bathroom. And a 4) _____ of the sea if possible.

Receptionist: I can give you the Blue Room, madam. It's en suite, overlooking the sea. What time will you 5) _____ in?

Customer: We'll be arriving at about 4.30 in the afternoon.

Receptionist: And would you like 6) _____ board – that's dinner, bed and breakfast?

Customer: Yes, please. Do you accept 7) _____ cards? Visa?

Receptionist: No problem, madam. May I take your card number now, to 8) _____ your reservation? And your name, please?

Using public transport

station	single ticket	passenger	luggage
ticket office	day return	the elderly	lost property
timetable	weekend return	the disabled	waiting room
book (in advance)	season ticket	driver	no smoking
fare	student reduction	inspector	
		express	

I'd like a day return to Cardiff.   You need to change buses / trains in Birmingham.

Bus

bus stop   bus shelter
coach   double-decker
upstairs   downstairs
conductor   bus station

How often does the number 73 run?

Train

underground   the Tube (in London)
platform   guard   porter
compartment   carriage
buffet car   railway station

The trains aren't running on time.
The Bristol train is delayed / cancelled.

A Match the words 1–12 with the categories BUS, TRAIN or BOTH.

1 platform
2 compartment
3 shelter
4 conductor
5 carriage
6 station

7 season ticket
8 buffet car
9 inspector
10 guard
11 passenger
12 fare

BUS

TRAIN

BOTH

B Choose the correct word from the pair in brackets to complete the sentences.

1 Could you tell me how much the _____ to Churchill Square is? (fare / ticket)

2 I'm getting off the bus at the next _____ . (stop / station)

3 To get to the supermarket you need to take the number 5 _____ . (coach / bus)

4 Don't speak to the _____ while he's in charge of the bus – he might have an accident! (conductor / driver)

5 I'm sorry, the Glasgow train is _____ late. (running / driving)

6 From a distance we counted twelve _____ on the train, as it went up the hill. (carriages / compartments)

C Look at the situations and respond, using expressions from the study box.

1 You want to go to London for the day by train. Ask for a ticket at the ticket office.

2 You want to know if you can smoke anywhere on the train.

3 You want to know if this bus goes to Redhill station.

4 You get on a bus, and sit down near the door, and wonder if the seat is specially for the old or people who have difficulty walking. Ask another passenger.

5 You want to know where to wait for the train to Exeter.

6 You would like to buy a ticket which allows you to travel the same route every day for a year.

Telephoning

call / ring / phone   dial a number   answer the phone   operator   extension
hold on / hold the line   put someone through   call back / try again later
ring off / hang up   engaged   answerphone / voicemail   wrong number

leave / take a message   give someone a message   send a text message / text someone
mobile (phone)   keypad   code   tone   telephone directory / phone book

Could I speak to ... ?   Who's calling, please?   This is Jane Russell.
I'm afraid he isn't here / available at the moment. Can I help?
I'm sorry, she's in a meeting / out of the office / away on business.

Can I take a message / Would you like to leave a message?
You could try calling him on his mobile.
Would you like to speak to his secretary?
His line's busy. Would you like to hold?

Please leave a message after the tone.   Press 2 on your keypad now.

A Match the questions or requests with the answers. Use each item only once.

1 Could I speak to Keith?
2 Operator, I dialled the number but nothing happened.
3 Can I make an appointment for Friday?
4 Is that Preston Library?
5 What's the code for Venezuela?
6 When will Mr Townsend be back?
7 Hold on a moment, please.
8 Can I have extension 42, please?

A Probably by Monday.
B You dial 0058, I think.
C Yes sir. I'm putting you through.
D I'm sorry, he isn't available.
E No, I'm sorry, I can't wait. I'll ring back later.
F Don't worry, I'll put the call through for you myself.
G Certainly. Would 2 o'clock be OK?
H No, I think you must have the wrong number.

B Complete the telephone conversation with words from the study box.

A Good morning, could I 1) _____ to Mr Philips, please?
B I'm 2) _____ , he isn't here at the 3) _____ .
A Could you give him a 4) _____ for me?
B Of course.
A Just tell him Robert called. I'll 5) _____ him again next week.
B I'll tell him. Goodbye.
A Thank you. Goodbye.

C Some of these definitions are not correct. Tick (✔) the right ones, and correct the wrong ones.

1 extension: an extra phone connected to the main phone line
2 operator: a person who repairs phones
3 to dial: to find a phone number in the directory
4 telephone directory: a book with people's phone numbers in it
5 engaged: busy, not available

UNIT 68

Shopping

<table>
<tr><td colspan="2">Food</td><td colspan="2">Clothes</td></tr>
<tr><td>supermarket</td><td>corner shop</td><td>department store</td><td>boutique</td></tr>
<tr><td>checkout</td><td>counter</td><td>fitting room</td><td>designer label</td></tr>
<tr><td>trolley</td><td>carrier bag</td><td>try on</td><td>second-hand</td></tr>
<tr><td>shelf</td><td>basket</td><td>sale</td><td>size</td></tr>
</table>

cheap   expensive   good value   a real bargain   in stock
pay in cash   pay by cheque   pay by credit card   pay with a store card

A Can I help you, madam?   B No, thanks. I'm just looking.
A How much is it?   B That comes to £15.50 altogether.

A Complete the conversation with words from the study box.

A Excuse me, could I 1) _____ on this dress?

B Certainly, madam, the 2) _____ room's over there.

A Right. It looks a bit small, you see, and I'm not sure of my 3) _____ .

B Well, just let me know, madam. I can always bring you a larger one, if you like.

A It's a real 4) _____ , isn't it? Very cheap!

B Yes, it's in our summer 5) _____ .

B Choose the correct word(s) from the pair in brackets to complete the sentences.

1 We need some more vegetables. I'll have to go to the _____ . (supermarket / department store)

2 Would you like to try _____ those trousers?   (on / out)

3 You can get the bread and I'll get the milk. See you at the _____ . (shelf / checkout)

4 Here is the jacket and your receipt, sir. Shall I put it in a _____ for you?   (trolley / carrier bag)

5 I can only afford designer clothes if I buy them _____ . (used / second-hand)

6 Have you got any more shirts like this in _____ ?   (stock / shop)

C Look at the situations and respond, using expressions from the study box.

1 A shop assistant says to you, 'Can I help you?' You don't need any help and you aren't sure what you want.

2 In a department store, you like the look of a pair of trousers, but you don't know if they will fit you. Ask an assistant for help.

3 You want to know if the boutique where you are shopping will accept a credit card.

4 Someone asks you, 'Where do you get the freshest, cheapest food? At a supermarket or a little corner shop?' Give your opinion.

5 Someone asks you, 'Where do you usually buy your clothes? At a department store, or a boutique, or a second-hand shop?' Give your opinion.

UNIT 69

Instructions and processes

---

plug it in   switch / turn it on   switch / turn it off   unplug it
press the button / switch / key   turn the dial / knob / handle to the left / right
turn it clockwise / anti-clockwise   pull it towards you   push it away from you

How do you set the timer?   What do you do next?   What do you do if ...?
What happens when you press this?   The television won't work / isn't working!
Insert the tape and select the correct channel.

Make sure it's plugged in.   Key in the correct 4-digit code.
Check the number / setting on the display panel.
Put some money / your card in the slot.

The tomatoes are sorted by machine, then cooked in giant ovens before being packed.

A Choose the correct word from the pair in brackets to complete the sentences.

1 To open the door, put the key in the lock and then _____ it. (switch / turn)

2 The herbs are _____ to the oil, and then the mixture _____ heated. (adding / added, is / are)

3 If you want to watch something on television, just _____ the button and then you can use the remote control. (press / switch)

4 Turn the _____ to the right. (button / dial) That's _____ . (clockwise / anti-clockwise)

5 The door's quite difficult to open. Try _____ it towards you while you _____ the handle.   (pushing / pulling, unplug / turn)

B Complete the instructions, using words from the study box.

If you get to the office early, the photocopier may be off. So you should 1) _____ it on, and wait for it to warm up.

If you spend all your money shopping on Saturday, you can always get some more cash from a cashpoint machine. You know, you can often find one outside a bank. You have to put your 2) _____ in the slot, 3) _____ some buttons, and hope you get the money!

Do you want to borrow my mobile phone? Just switch it 4) _____ here and 5) _____ the number. Is it ringing?

We need to pay in this car park. Can you get a ticket from the machine over there, please? Just 6) _____ some money in the 7) _____, and press the green 8) _____ .

C Look at the situations and respond, using expressions from the study box.

1 Someone in the room says, 'It's cold in here! I don't think the heating's on.' Offer to help.

2 A friend complains, 'My DVD player isn't working!'

3 Someone says, 'I wonder where they make Seats.' You know that Seat is a Spanish car company.

4 Another friend asks, 'What do you do about your heating and electricity if you go away on holiday?'

Agreeing and disagreeing

Agreeing
That's what I think.   I quite agree with you.   You're absolutely right.
Oh yes, I agree.   You're quite right.   That's very true.   I think so too.

Undecided
It depends what you mean.   That may sometimes be true.
*I'm not sure about that.   What do **you** think about it?   I don't know.*

Disagreeing
I'm sorry, I can't agree with that.   Well, that's true, but ...   I don't agree.
You have a point, but ...   I don't think that's quite right.
I really can't agree with you.   I'm sure you've got the wrong idea about ...

A Michelle is thinking about looking for another job, and is discussing this with her friends James and Heidi. Look at their conversation, and decide whether they are agreeing or disagreeing with each other, or are undecided. Write A (for agreeing), D (for disagreeing) or U (for undecided).

James:	I think you're right to leave the company, Michelle.	1 ____
Michelle:	Do you? I'm not sure.	2 ____
Heidi:	James, I really can't agree with you.	3 ____
James:	Look, Michelle isn't happy, so she should leave!	4 ____
Heidi:	You have a point there, but what about money?	5 ____
Michelle:	Yes, you're absolutely right, Heidi. I really need my salary at the moment.	6 ____
James:	Well, that's true, but you'll find another job soon.	7 ____
Heidi:	It depends. Jobs aren't easy to find now.	8 ____
Michelle:	Oh, dear! I just don't know what to do.	9 ____

B Look at the statements and decide what you think about them. Then discuss them with a partner, or write down your opinions, using expressions from the study box.

1 Watching television is just a waste of time.
2 Basketball is the most exciting sport in the world.
3 Learning English is fun!
4 Animals feel as much as humans.
5 Men and women should be allowed to do the same jobs.
6 It's better to go to work by bus than by car.
7 Classical music is only for old people.

C Look at the situations and respond, using expressions from the study box

1 A friend of your father's says, 'All school children should wear uniforms.'
2 Your uncle says, 'Anyone who receives a present should always write a thank-you letter.'
3 A friend says, 'The King's Club is the best disco in town.'
4 Your sister says, 'Our team isn't playing well enough. They won't win the championship!'
5 Someone you don't know well says, 'Ugh! Dark green! I hate that colour, don't you?'
6 Your mother says, 'Wasn't that a wonderful holiday we had last year?'

Thanking and apologising

Thanks

Thank you so much. How kind of you!
Thank you very much. That is kind of you!
Thanks very much indeed. I am grateful.
Thank you for having me.
Thank you for a lovely weekend.
Thank you so much for all your help.

Apologies

I'm so sorry.   I'm terribly sorry.
I really am sorry.   I'm really sorry.
I'm awfully sorry. It was an accident.
It was all my fault. It was a mistake.
It won't happen again, I promise.
I didn't mean to do it. I do apologise.

Replies

Don't mention it.   My pleasure.   It was no trouble.   You're welcome.
Never mind.   It doesn't matter.   Don't worry about it.   That's all right.

A Match the thanks and apologies with the replies. Use each item only once.

1 Thanks for helping me.
2 I'm sorry about the dirt.
3 I *do* apologise for her rudeness.
4 I *am* grateful for the flowers.
5 Thanks for taking me home.
6 It was all my fault.
7 How kind of you to buy him a present!
8 I'm sorry I broke the cup.

A Don't mention it. He's a good boy.
B That's all right. I can mend it.
C It doesn't matter. I can still drive it.
D It was no trouble. I *like* helping people!
E Don't worry, she's always like that.
F You're welcome. It's on my way.
G Never mind. I'll soon get it clean.
H My pleasure. I know you like roses.

B Look at the situations and respond, using expressions from the study box.

1 You have been staying with friends for the weekend, and you're just about to leave. You've had a lovely time.
2 Someone on a crowded bus has just tripped over your foot, and is now lying on the floor. Apologise, and try to explain that you didn't mean to trip them up.
3 You were daydreaming while shopping, and took something out of a shop without paying. The store detective accuses you of stealing.
4 After a short holiday you arrive home at your local airport. You are delighted because a friend has unexpectedly come to collect you by car.
5 A friend has been extremely helpful with a school project you've been doing recently. Make sure you thank him or her properly.
6 While out driving your father's car, you unfortunately bump into another car. There isn't much damage, but you apologise to the other driver, and, later, to your father.
7 Someone lent you some money last week when you needed some desperately. Now you are returning it, with thanks.
8 You were supposed to ring your girl / boyfriend last night, but you were watching a fantastic film on television. Apologise to her or him.

Asking permission

Requests

May I leave?   Can I go out?   Could I borrow that?
Do you mind if I smoke?   Would you mind if I didn't come?
Could I possibly have a key?   Do you think I could see the manager?
Would it be all right if I went home now?

Replies

Well, I'm not sure.   No, I'm afraid you can't.   Of course (not).
I'd rather you didn't.   Certainly.   You may.   You can.
Yes, that's all right.   Yes, I think so.   Help yourself.
Not at all, please do.   Not at all, go ahead.   No problem, it's up to you.

A Match the requests with the replies. Use each item only once.

1 May I use a dictionary?   A Not at all, please do.

2 Could I borrow the car tonight?   B You may, but it must be English–English!

3 Can I see the director?   C Yes, if you put some petrol in.

4 Could I have an extra lesson?   D I'd rather you didn't. Phoning is very expensive here.

5 Would you mind if I used your phone?   E Certainly. How about Friday?

6 Do you mind if I sit down?   F Yes, I think so, if he's in.

B Look at the situations and respond, using expressions from the study box.

1 You are staying with a friend but you've forgotten to bring your hairdryer. Ask your friend.

2 You would like to have your supper early so that you can go out with your friends. Ask the person who usually cooks your supper.

3 You would like to borrow a book your friend has been reading. Ask him or her.

4 You need to ask your teacher if you can leave class early to go to the dentist.

5 You don't feel well. Ask for permission to go home immediately.

6 You are on a plane, and would like a vegetarian meal, instead of the meat or fish. Ask the steward or stewardess.

7 You need to borrow a friend's bike to get to the post office before it closes. Ask your friend.

8 Your friend asks, 'Could I borrow your camera for the weekend?' It cost you a lot of money, and your friend isn't always very careful with things!

9 In the street, a stranger says, 'We're doing a survey. Would you mind if I asked you some questions?' You have plenty of time and like answering questions.

10 Someone asks you, 'Can I park here?' You know parking is not allowed there.

Suggesting

These are all ways of suggesting an idea or a plan:

We could go by bus or by taxi.
Why don't we go sailing tomorrow?
How about getting tickets for that musical?
What about working together on the project?
Let's wait and see.
Should we have a picnic?
Shall we take your car?

Note that you must use the **-ing** form after How about / What about ...?
and a question mark at the end of the sentence if you start with
Why don't we / How about / What about / Shall we / Should we ...?

A Choose the correct ending A, B or C to complete the suggestions.

1 Let's ____
2 Why don't we ____
3 We could ____
4 What about ____
5 Should we ____
6 Shall we ____
7 How about ____

A travelling by air?

B take a taxi.

C go by bus?

B Choose the correct word from the pair in brackets to complete the sentences.

1 Should we _____ the police? I think we should.   (tell / telling)
2 Let's _____ down to the beach for a swim. (go / going)
3 We could _____ our supper later. What do you think? (have / having)
4 Why don't we _____ a few more photos? I've got another roll of film. (take / taking)
5 What about _____ the cassettes after school? (buy / buying)
6 Shall we _____ the doctor's opinion? He'll be here soon. (ask / asking)
7 How about _____ a video tonight? (watch / watching)
8 Why don't you _____ Marlene a birthday present? (get / getting)
9 What about _____ out at the weekend? (eat / eating)
10 Let's _____ a camping holiday this year. (try / trying)

C Make suggestions to a friend who ...

1 ... has no money left for the rest of this month.
2 ... has broken his / her landlady's window.
3 ... has decided to come and stay with you for a weekend.
4 ... wants to go on holiday with you.

Interrupting and changing the topic

Interrupting	Changing the topic
Excuse me, can I come in?	*By the way, have you ever skied in Colorado?*
Excuse me, could you pass me the bread?	*That reminds me – did we turn the water off?*
Could I just say something at this point?	*Oh, I see. And what about your new job?*
Sorry to break in, but this is delicious!	*Oh, right. And what news of Julia these days?*
Sorry, could you explain how this works?	*And another thing – who's paying for the food?*

A Match the beginnings and endings of these interruptions.

1 Excuse me, can
2 Could I just
3 Sorry to break in,
4 Excuse me, I think it's
5 Sorry, could you

A but surely that's wrong.
B my turn now.
C give me a hand with this?
D say what I think here?
E I join the guided tour?

B Put this conversation between two friends in the correct order.

a *Felicity*: Yes, thanks. Martin and I went to Paris, actually. We had a wonderful time.
b *Sandra*: Oh dear! And what about your mother – is she better now?
c *Felicity*: Hi there, did you have a good weekend?
d *Sandra*: Lucky you! That reminds me, did you see that French film on TV last night?
e *Felicity*: Yes, she's out of hospital, thank goodness.
f *Sandra*: Yes, it was great. Did you?
g *Felicity*: No, it was on too late and I forgot to record it.

C Complete the four parts of conversations with words from the study box.

1 *A* Yes, we really loved Egypt.
   B By the _____ , have you ever been to Mexico?

2 *A* I hear that Sven is marrying Louise.
   B Oh, right. What _____ of Anna these days?

3 *A* And then I told the professor …
   B Sorry to _____ in, but didn't *he* tell *you*?

4 *A* It rained and rained, and so I …
   B _____ me, can I just say something?

D Look at the situations and respond, using expressions from the study box.

1 You don't know how to use a drinks machine at a sports centre. Two of the centre's employees are talking to each other nearby. Interrupt them (politely!) and ask for help.

2 A friend of yours is talking about his studies at university. Change the topic, and get him to talk about a party you and he are planning to give together.

3 You are having dinner at your sister's house. She is talking about a problem with her computer. Interrupt her to tell her how good the food is. Or change the topic, and tell her about a problem you're having with your mobile phone.

Inviting, refusing and accepting

Inviting

Can you come to lunch?   Do come to the barbecue!
Would you like to have dinner with me?
Will you come to my party?
I'd like you to come to dinner. (semi-formal)
I would like to invite you to the reception. (formal)

Refusing

I'm sorry, I can't that day.   What a pity! I can't make it.
I'm afraid I'm very busy that week.   I don't think I can.
*Oh, I **am** sorry. I won't be able to.*
I'm afraid I'm unable to come.
I regret I am unable to accept. (formal)

Accepting

I'd love to. What time?   Yes, that would be lovely.   Great! What fun!
Yes, I think so. When exactly?   Yes, I'll look forward to it.
I would be delighted to accept. (formal)

A Choose the correct word(s) from the pair in brackets to complete the sentences.

1 _____ you come to the meeting?   (May / Will)

2 Would you _____ to play tennis with me? (like / love)

3 I'm _____ , I can't come then. (afraid / sorry)

4 What a pity! I won't be able _____ . (it / to)

5 Great! We'll _____ forward to it. (look / looking)

6 Gerald, _____ like you to come to lunch. (I'd / I)

7 I regret I am _____ to accept. (can't / unable)

8 I'd love to come. What _____ ! (funny / fun)

9 Yes, that would be _____ . (delighted / lovely)

10 He'd like _____ and see him. (that you go / you to go)

B Look at the situations and respond, using expressions from the study box.

1 You're going to celebrate your eighteenth birthday with a big party in two weeks' time. Invite your friends.

2 Your best friend invites you to go on an exciting weekend trip with him / her. You accept.

3 Your aunt invites you to spend a few days at her house, but you've already arranged something for that week, so you will have to refuse.

4 Invite someone you don't know very well to have a meal with you and your family.

5 A friend rings up and says, 'How about coming round to my place tonight, to listen to some music?' You have too much homework!

6 Your boss invites you to a barbecue at his house on Saturday. You accept politely.

Giving advice and warnings

<table>
<tr><td>

Advice

If I were you, I'd go home.

If I were you, I wouldn't worry.

I think you ought to / should take an aspirin.

I don't think you should do that.

You shouldn't go to bed so late.

I advise you to think about it.

My advice is to forget about it.

</td><td>

Warnings

If you don't study harder, you'll fail the test.

Don't shout so loud, or you'll wake the baby.

If you do that again, you'll be sorry!

There'll be trouble if you go on like this.

You'd better go now. Otherwise you'll be late.

Be careful when you cross the road.

Watch out! There's a snake near your foot.

</td></tr>
</table>

A Choose the correct word(s) from the pair in brackets to complete the sentences.

1 Don't cry, _____ you'll have red eyes.   (if / or)

2 Watch _____ ! There's a car coming very fast.   (out / up)

3 You _____ to tell me what happened.   (ought / should)

4 If you say you're sorry, _____ forgive you.   (I'll / I'm)

5 I think you _____ buy her some flowers.   (must / should)

6 If I _____ you, I wouldn't mind.   (are / were)

7 My _____ is to phone the police at once.   (advice / advise)

8 You'd _____ go home, or there'll be trouble.   (rather / better)

9 If you _____ get more sleep, you'll make yourself ill.   (do / don't)

10 If you drive on the other side of the road, be _____ .
(carefully / careful)

B Look at the situations and respond, using expressions from the study box.

1 A friend says, 'I've broken my mother's favourite teapot. What shall I do?'

2 Your little sister says, 'I don't think my friends at school really like me!' What advice can you give?

3 Your young brother says, 'I really want to pass the exam next week, but I haven't done much studying so far. What can I do?'

4 Your best friend goes out every evening, and doesn't have enough time for homework. You are worried this is going to be a problem. Give him / her some good advice.

5 Your little cousin is running into the kitchen. Someone has just washed the floor. You don't want him to slip, so what do you say?

6 Someone you know often tells lies. Other people are beginning to notice. Warn him / her what will happen unless he / she changes and becomes more truthful.

7 Someone in your class looks very white and ill. What helpful advice can you give?

8 You go into a very old café with a friend of yours, who is rather tall. The ceiling is low, and you suddenly notice your friend is about to hit his head on it. How can you warn him?

Complaining

Could I speak to the manager? *I'd like to return this.* *It's faulty.*
I'm afraid this isn't working. *I can't make it work.* *It doesn't seem to work.*
There's something wrong with it. *It's poor quality.* *It's much too expensive.*
I'm afraid the service wasn't very good. *The food was cold / tasteless / greasy / stale.*

a receipt a replacement a refund / your money back

Could you replace it, please? *Can I have a refund / my money back, please?*
I'd like you to pay me compensation. *I'm not happy with the food / service / goods.*
I refuse to pay the bill / invoice until you repair it / put it right / replace it.

A Complete the conversation with words from the study box.

A Good morning, I'd like to 1) _____ this mobile phone to you.

B What's 2) _____ with it, sir?

A Well, it doesn't 3) _____ to work.

B I'm so sorry, sir. Have you got the 4) _____ , to show that you bought it here?

A Yes, here it is. I bought it yesterday.

B Would you like a 5) _____ , sir? We have lots more in stock.

A No, thank you. I'd like my money back.

B I'm sorry, sir. We never give a 6) _____ on mobile phones.

A We'll see about that! Can I speak to the 7) _____ , please?

B Certainly. This way, sir.

B Look at the situations and respond, using expressions from the study box.

1 You buy a television, but when you switch on, the screen is blank. Ring up the shop to complain.

2 You've just finished a meal in a restaurant with some friends. The steak was tough, the vegetables overcooked, and the chips greasy. Complain to the waiter.

3 A photographic shop developed your holiday photos, but the colours don't look right to you. Complain to the manager.

4 Your hairdresser has accidentally turned your hair green! Refuse to pay until he / she has changed it back to your normal colour.

5 You bought some fish from a supermarket, but it smells bad. Take it back and ask for a refund.

6 You've just asked about information at the bus station, but the staff there never smile or take any interest in people. Complain to the manager.

7 You had a really awful holiday at a hotel recommended by a travel agent. Complain and ask for a refund and compensation for your ruined holiday.

8 You bought a book, but now you realise several pages are missing. Take it back to the bookshop for a replacement.

Spelling

> We use **capital letters** for the first word in a sentence, days of the week, months, countries, languages, nationalities, names of places and people, and titles:
> * *Monday, April, Jordan, Dutch, the Equator, Belfast, Professor Warburton*

A Use capital letters in the text wherever you think they are necessary.

some years ago, in the month of june, two men arrived at the north pole. their names were professor donald shawcross and doctor jeff thomas. for twelve days they had walked across a thousand miles of ice, carrying or pulling all their food and equipment. they were both canadian, and had done their training in alaska and the rocky mountains.

> Here is a useful spelling rule: **i** before **e** except after **c**, with some exceptions.

B Underline the correct spelling. (There are no exceptions.)

1 freind / friend
2 receive / recieve
3 beleive / believe
4 theif / thief
5 niece / neice

6 chief / cheif
7 receipt / reciept
8 deceive / decieve
9 field / feild
10 ceiling / cieling

> Most nouns in English add **-s** in the plural, but there are many where you can't do this:
>
> | child ~ children | man ~ men | woman ~ women |
> |---|---|---|
> | foot ~ feet | mouse ~ mice | tooth ~ teeth |
> | deer ~ deer | sheep ~ sheep | fish ~ fish |
> | leaf ~ leaves | wolf ~ wolves | knife ~ knives |
> | potato ~ potatoes | tomato ~ tomatoes | hero ~ heroes |
> | pony ~ ponies | penny ~ pennies | family ~ families |
> | bus ~ buses | glass ~ glasses | beach ~ beaches |

C Give the correct plural for these words.

1 potato
2 child
3 foot
4 sheep

5 bus
6 wolf
7 family
8 hero

9 knife
10 fish
11 mouse
12 woman

If you add **-er** or **-ed** or **-ing** to a short word, you usually double the last letter:

• *drip ~ dripping   run ~ running   fat ~ fatter   thin ~ thinner   stop ~ stopped*

but only if it is a short sound, not a long one often ending in **-e**:

• *wave ~ waving   hope ~ hoping   phone ~ phoning   write ~ writing
take ~ taking*

D Some of these spellings are not correct. Tick (✔) the right ones, and correct the wrong ones.

1 runing	5 geting	9 claping	13 biger
2 flapped	6 travelled	10 hitting	14 faster
3 wavving	7 dropping	11 promised	15 hoping
4 becomming	8 looked	12 driping	16 shoping

Watch out for these **easily-confused groups of words**:

• *too, two, to* • *they're, their, there* • *where, were* • *write, right*
• *princes, princess* • *know, now, no* • *your, you're* • *four, for*
• *here, hear*

and these **silent letters**:

• *clim**b**   **h**andsome   forei**g**n   **h**our   **k**nife   cal**m**   cu**p**board   **h**orse
cas**t**le   **w**rite*

Remember – *beauti**ful**, grace**ful**, help**ful**, use**ful** but the glass was **full** of water.*

E Correct the spelling in the text. There are twenty-one mistakes. See if you can find them all!

Once upon a time their was a princes, who lived in a casle. She was an intelligent and beautifull girl with long blonde heir, but she was lonely because she had know freinds. One day wen she was riting a letter, she heared a shout from below her window. She ran to look out, and saw a hansome young prince outside on his hoarse.
'Come four a ride with me!' he said. 'Your to lovely to stay at home alone!'
'Perhaps,' she said. She wasn't sure.
'I love you!' he said. 'Don't you beleive me?'
She went to the cuboard, found a nife and cut off her long hair. She made it into a rope, and climed out of the window.
'Hear I am!' she said.
'I no we'll be happy together!' said the prince, and they rode away.

F These words are often spelt wrongly, and some of them are not correct here.
Tick (✔) the right ones and correct the wrong ones.

1 advertisment	6 sader	11 realy	16 misstake
2 accomodation	7 necesary	12 cheap	17 appartment
3 begining	8 building	13 buisness	18 colledge
4 storys	9 company	14 polise	19 happier
5 confortable	10 jorney	15 holliday	20 exept

Postcards

When you write a **postcard,** make sure the address of the person you are writing to is very clear. When you write your message, you do not need to use complete sentences. Most postcards are written in **informal** style, with short forms, like *doesn't, I'm, you're, won't.*

Use a suitable **ending**: *Regards* or *Yours* for someone you do not know well, ***Best wishes*** for a friend, and *Love* for a close friend.
Look at the postcard layout below.

place and date

name of the person you are writing to

Dear + person's name

Barcelona, 19.7.04

Dear Ros,
Having a great time here. It's been sunny every day so far. Hope you are well. Wish you were here!

Your message

Mrs R. North
7 Mayle Drive
Newcastle-under-Lyme
Staffordshire
ST5 8RS
ENGLAND

number and street

county (if you know it)

postcode

country (if necessary)

ending + your name

Love,
Sylvia

A Think what the following adjectives mean, and then put them into two lists according to whether they are 'good' or 'bad'.

super   wonderful   terrible   awful   crowded   miserable   disgusting   exciting   changeable   busy   great   cold   noisy   excellent   delicious   unpleasant

GOOD: _____

BAD: _____

B How many weather adjectives do you know? Make adjectives to describe the weather from the nouns.

1	cloud	_____	6	rain	_____
2	fog	_____	7	snow	_____
3	frost	_____	8	sun	_____
4	ice	_____	9	thunder	_____
5	mist	_____	10	wind	_____

Now use the most suitable ones to complete the sentences.

11 The road was white and _____ this morning, although there wasn't any snow.

12 It was so _____ on the motorway that we couldn't see where we were going.

13 Some countries have a dry season and a _____ season.

14 The weather last July was warm and _____ , so the children swam in the sea every day.

15 Pete's dog really hates _____ weather – it doesn't like the sudden noise!

C Put the names and the parts of addresses in the right order.

1 London, Southwick Street, Highways Agency, 890-898, SE1 0TE

2 EX8 3TS, Paul Holmes, Church Street, 12, Exmouth

3 Flat 7, Brighton, Sillwood House, Barbara Wilson, Sillwood Street, BN1 7BC

4 Lindfield Close, OX3 8PR, Edward Canham, Oxford, 72

5 Scotland, 20, EH5 1SA, Mayborn Way, Edinburgh, Ahmed Hadi

6 196, Tony Griffiths, Shrewsbury, Woodland Drive, SY2 3AB

7 York, North Road, Jane Campbell, Yorkshire, 25, YO1 8TG

8 West Avenue, HP20 5BP, Ken Lambert, 6A, Aylesbury

D Correct the postcard. There are twelve mistakes in it.

Dear my friend,
This is beautiful place. I very happy here. The sun shine every day. Yesterday I go to see the king's palace. Who are you? Maybe next year we have holiday together.
Write me soon.
Best wish,
Georg

Giuseppe Visconti
Duke Street 20
OX2 8ES
Oxford

E Write one or more of these postcards, using 35–45 words. Look at the study box and the Ten Writing Tips on page 127 before you start.

1 You are on holiday in Brazil / Ireland / New Zealand / the Caribbean / the French Alps. Write a postcard to an English friend of yours. In your card,
   • explain where you are
   • describe the weather
   • say what sightseeing you are planning to do.

2 You stayed for a weekend at a friend's house. Write a card to your friend's mother. In your card,
   • thank her for inviting you to stay
   • say how delicious the meals were
   • wish her and her family a nice summer holiday.

3 A friend has suggested going to a concert with you, and has sent you a list of concerts and dates. Write a card to your friend. In your card,
   • say which concert you prefer
   • offer to book the tickets
   • say how much you are looking forward to it.

E-mails and notes

> **E-mails** are electronic messages, usually sent via computers.
>
> If you send an e-mail to someone you don't know well, or your e-mail is about work:
> • use the correct beginning and ending
> • write complete sentences.
>
> If you send an e-mail to a friend or someone you know well:
> • you can use an informal greeting like *Hi* or *Hello* instead of *Dear*
> • you can write in an informal style
> • you don't need complete sentences
> • you can leave out small words like *it* or *the* and use short forms like *won't*.
>
> (See **Units 83** and **84** for beginnings and endings of letters.)

A Look at Pete's e-mail to his friend Nick, and read the sentences below. Are they true (T) or false (F)? Write **T** or **F** after each sentence. You may have to 'read between the lines'!

> Hi, Nick!
> Any chance of borrowing your car this weekend? Jane's thinking of going down south to see her parents – I could go along too if we had a car. Costs a fortune going all that way by train. But don't worry if you need it.
>
> See you,
> Pete

1 Jane is Nick's girlfriend.
2 Nick has already agreed to lend his car to Pete.
3 Jane's parents live nearby.
4 It's cheaper travelling by train than by car.

B Look at Nick's e-mail, replying to Pete. Put the parts of the e-mail in the right order.

a So I'll decide tomorrow and let you know.
b Hi, Pete!
c Say hello to Jane for me.
d I might need it on Saturday to get to a match.
e See you. Nick
f But if I'm not going to the match, then you can have it.

C Jane is sending an e-mail to her parents. What style of writing does she use? Choose the most suitable words or phrases each time.

1 To my dear parents: / Dear Mum and Dad,
2 May come and visit this weekend / We intend to visit you this weekend
3 if we can borrow a car / depending on whether a car is available.
4 Is that OK? / Please let me know your timetable.
5 Kind regards, Jane / Love, Jane

> **Notes** are messages or very short letters. In a note, you can
> - ask someone to do something
> - thank someone for something
> - give or accept or refuse an invitation
> - ask for or offer information
> - describe something for sale
> - describe something you have lost
> - apologise for something.
>
> Make sure your message is clear, and keep it short. Put your name or initial(s) at the end of a note.

D Complete these three notes, writing **one** word in each space.

1 Julie

Borrowed £10 to _____ some food. Will _____ you back tonight.
Christine

2 Mr Marshall rang. Is hoping to _____ from you very _____ .
Can you phone him _____ you get in?
Bill

3
> **For sale**
>
> Mountain _____ , good condition, tyres _____ replacing.
> Only 2 years _____ , reasonable _____ .
> Phone Sam on 07784-233554

E Write one or more of these e-mails or notes, using 35–45 words. Look at the study box and the Ten Writing Tips on page 127 before you start.

1 You are going to start a new job next week. Write an e-mail to an Australian friend of yours. In your e-mail,
- explain what kind of job it is
- say why you wanted to leave your old job
- give your new contact details at work.

2 While trying to park your car, you have bumped into someone else's car and caused some damage. Write a note to leave on the other person's car. In your note,
- apologise for damaging the car
- promise to pay for the repair (or get your insurance company to pay)
- give your name and phone number.

3 You want to find out some information about a rock band who made some records a few years ago. Write an e-mail to a friend who knows a lot about rock music. In your e-mail,
- say what information you are looking for
- explain why you want to know this
- thank your friend in advance for helping you.

Filling in forms

You will find these words and phrases useful:
First name / Forename   Family name / Surname   Occupation
Title   Sex   Age   Height   Nationality
Marital status   Date and country of birth
Address   Postcode   Phone number (daytime / evening)
Signature   Block capitals   Initials   Tick (✓)   Cross (✗)

A Match the words 1–10 with the information. Use each item only once.

1	Title	A	21 / 65 / 72 / 34
2	Age	B	Donizetti / Onassis / Henderson
3	Occupation	C	Male / Female
4	Sex	D	Italy / Spain / Kuwait
5	Nationality	E	Professor / Mr / Mrs / Dr / Ms / Miss
6	First name	F	Single / Married / Divorced / Widowed
7	Surname	G	1.67 m / 1.52 m
8	Marital status	H	Malik / Yuko / Tim
9	Country of birth	I	Japanese / Swiss / Nigerian
10	Height	J	Student / Teacher / Unemployed / Engineer

B Your friend Angela is not much good at filling in forms! Perhaps you can help her. See how many of her mistakes you can find and correct.

Complete this form in BLOCK CAPITALS. Put a tick in the correct boxes.

First name: *Hampton*   Surname: *Angela*

Title: *Single*   Initials: *ANGELA*

Sex: Male ☐   Female ✗   Marital status: *I have a boyfriend.*

Age: *17.06.80*   Height: *52 kilos*

Occupation: *I like reading.*   Nationality: *Canada*

Country of birth: *Canadian*   Place of birth: *PARIS*

Address: *10 Hawkhurst Road, NE20 3TS*

_____ Postcode: *London*

Do you speak other languages?   Yes ☐   No ✗

How many countries have you visited? One ☐   More than one ✗

Can you drive a car?   Yes ✗   No ☐

Signature: *ANGELA HAMPTON*   Date: *17.06.80*

C Fill in these forms.

Here's your chance to make the friends you've always wanted, or even to meet the partner of your dreams!

Simply complete this questionnaire and send it to us. We'll do the rest! As soon as we receive your form, we'll send you, completely free, the name and short description of someone who could be the perfect person for you. If you want to join Heartline and receive lots more names and addresses, just send a cheque for £20 with the form you'll find in our letter. You'll never regret it!

Please use block capitals.

1

Mr ☐ Mrs ☐ Miss ☐ Ms ☐

Surname_____

First name_____

Address _____

Postcode_____

Phone number _____

E-mail address _____

2

Your marital status _____

Your age _____ Your height ____

Your occupation _____

Your character (tick box):

Serious ☐ Romantic ☐

Generous ☐ Careful ☐

Practical ☐ A dreamer ☐

Shy ☐ Sociable ☐

3

Your interests (tick box):

Sports ☐ Music ☐

Travelling ☐ Cinema ☐

Walking ☐ Dancing ☐

Theatre ☐ Animals ☐

Reading ☐ Computers ☐

4

Your ideas about life (tick box):

Do you prefer living in towns? Yes ☐ No ☐

Do you like working with / being with other people? Yes ☐ No ☐

Do you want to make a lot more new friends? Yes ☐ No ☐

Have you known your friends for a long time? Yes ☐ No ☐

Do you like going out every evening? Yes ☐ No ☐

5

Details of the people you want to meet:

Age _____ Height _____

Occupation _____

Character (tick box):

Serious ☐ Romantic ☐

Generous ☐ Careful ☐

Practical ☐ A dreamer ☐

Shy ☐ Sociable ☐

Thank you for booking an English language course with the Lion School, Oxford.
Please fill in this form, as we need the following information for our files:

First name _____ Marital status _____

Surname _____ Occupation _____

Sex (tick) Male ☐ Female ☐ Nationality _____

Address _____

_____ Postcode _____

Date & place of birth _____

Phone number (daytime) _____ (evening) _____

Do you want to stay with an English family? _____

Which exams do you want to take?_____

What are the exact dates of your stay at the Lion School? _____

Signature_____ Date_____

Sentence building

These **linking words** are often used to join parts of sentences:

and	but	or	either ... or ...
when	until	before	after
where	although	while	during
because	since	as	for
so	so that	(in order) to	as soon as

He stayed until the restaurant closed.   *I'll phone as soon as I arrive.*
Although it was hot, we went for a walk.   *While I was in Belgium, I learnt French.*
She studied hard, but she didn't pass all her exams.   *I'll come when I can.*
During my illness I wrote a short story.   *He went home after doing the shopping.*
Because / Since / As you're my friend, I trust you.   *We could either eat out or stay in.*
She was ill, so she stayed in bed.
He saved some money (in order) to pay for a holiday / so that he could pay for a holiday.

Look back at **Unit 29** for an explanation of some of these linking words.

A Choose the correct word(s) from the pair in brackets to complete the sentences.

1 Wait here _____ your parents arrive.   (until / while)

2 Ramon studied hard _____ his holiday.   (while / during)

3 I haven't seen Rolf _____ ten years.   (for / since)

4 Heidi went to Tunis _____ study there.   (in order to / so that)

5 Stella lent us a lot of money, _____ we had a wonderful time!
(so / that)

6 I don't like beef, _____ I *do* like chicken.   (or / but)

7 I'll ring Andrea _____ I can.   (until / as soon as)

8 Alicia travelled by coach, _____ it was the cheapest way.
(while / because)

9 _____ Antonio has lots of friends, he doesn't go out much.
(Although / But)

10 _____ *you* tell the teacher, or *I* will!   (Either / Or)

So ... that ... and **such ... that ...** are also important linking words:

• *She spoke so fast that we couldn't understand.*
• *It was such an interesting exercise that we enjoyed doing it.*

so + adjectives, adverbs, *much, many, little, few*
such + adjectives with nouns, *a lot of*

B Complete the sentences with *so* or *such*.

1 They were _____ intelligent people that they solved the problem.
2 There was _____ little money that the hospital had to close.
3 It was _____ a warm day that we had a swim.

4 There were _____ a lot of oranges that we decided to make some marmalade.

5 The old lady walked _____ slowly that it took her ten minutes to get home.

6 There were _____ few people that the show was cancelled.

7 It was _____ interesting news that we all stopped talking.

8 She's got _____ a lot of furniture that you can't see the carpet!

C Match the two halves of the sentences, and connect them with the following linking word(s): *because but   in order to so that until where while*

1 He was born in Barcelona,
2 I am writing to you
3 She was listening to the radio
4 Go straight on
5 Harold was a bank manager,
6 Magda was such a good hairdresser
7 Therese went on a diet,
8 Paco studied hard

A she was doing the ironing.
B he didn't have a credit card.
C he's lived all his life.
D enter university.
E she lost weight.
F I would like to apply for the job.
G she opened her own salon.
H you reach the crossroads.

D Complete the text, using the following linking word(s): *although and because but or so that until where while*

Sam went slowly upstairs to his room. He sat down at his desk, 1) _____ his pen, paper and books lay waiting for him. He felt tired 2) _____ knew he wasn't in the mood for homework. 'I'll listen to some music 3) _____ I feel better!' he thought. 4) _____ he turned on the radio. After twenty minutes, he turned it off, 5) _____ it wasn't the kind of music he liked. He looked again at his books. There was so much homework 6) _____ he couldn't do it all in one evening! 7) _____ he was thinking this, he began to feel hungry, 8) _____ he had only recently had supper. 'Shall I make a sandwich, 9) _____ just have an apple?' he wondered. He ate an apple, and then picked up his pen. 'Right!' he said to himself. 'It's difficult, 10) _____ I'm going to do it!'

E Correct the sentences.

1 Also I put some sun cream on, I still got burnt!
2 James learnt a lot while his stay in Uganda.
3 It was so a boring programme that Gavin fell asleep.
4 Daniela went to Kyoto for buying some presents.
5 Or they could say yes, or they could say no.
6 Write to me soon, therefore I can book the tickets.
7 She saved a lot of money, and she couldn't afford to go on holiday.
8 I'll ring him back until I get home.
9 He asked her to marry him, why he loved her.
10 Fiona had a shower after she went to bed.
11 Janie had a headache, so that she took an aspirin.
12 They were such kind people than we felt at home.

115

Formal letters

Be careful to use the correct style for a **formal letter**:

Dear Sir or Madam, → **Yours faithfully,** ...
Dear Mrs Wiggins, → **Yours sincerely,** ...

Thank you for your letter of 2nd August.

We would like to invite you to ...
I do apologise for not letting you know earlier ...
I would like to ask for more information ...
I would like to apply for the post of ...
I was not happy with the service I received ...
Could you tell me how much / how long / how far ...?
I look forward to receiving your reply / hearing from you soon.

Remember – do not use short forms in formal letters.

Sample task

You booked a weekend at a luxury hotel with three friends. Some time ago you decided to change your booking, but you forgot to inform the hotel. Now you are writing to the hotel (rather late!) to tell them about the change. Write a letter of about 100 words in formal style. Do not include addresses.

Dear Mrs Evans,

Thank you for your letter of 19th January, confirming my booking of two double rooms with private bathrooms for two nights in March.

I would like to inform you that my friends and I will not be arriving on Saturday 1st March, as planned, but on Saturday 8th March. **I do apologise for not letting you know earlier**. I hope this will not cause you any problems. Please let me know if there is any difficulty about this.

We are **looking forward to** our stay at your hotel.

Yours sincerely,

Pat Caplin

A Imagine you are going to write a letter in the following situations. Choose one sentence from the study box that you could include in each letter.

1 You want to have a camping holiday in the Highlands of Scotland, but you only know of one campsite. You are writing to the Scottish Tourist Office.

2 Your restaurant meal took a long time to arrive, and the waiter was rude. You want to complain to the manager.

3 There is a wonderful job advertised in the local paper. You are sure you could do it. You are writing to the manager of the company.

4 Your company has asked you to write to a number of possible customers, inviting them to a coffee morning.

5 You have come to the end of your letter. You hope the person you are writing to will write back very soon. What do you write?

B Put the parts of this formal letter in the right order.

a Yours faithfully,

b Thank you for your letter of 23rd May.

c but I have been very busy at work.

d Would Thursday be convenient for you?

e I look forward to receiving your reply.

f Dear Sir or Madam,

g I would be delighted to come to an interview,

h Rupert Jenkins

i I do apologise for not replying earlier,

j but I am afraid I cannot manage next Tuesday.

k I could come at any time on that day.

l You can phone, fax or e-mail me to let me know.

C Choose the expressions in the box which you can use in a formal letter, and underline them.

Dear friend,	See you soon,	Love from …
Write soon,	I look forward to …	I would like to apply …
Sorry I forgot …	Hi there!	Could you tell me …
I didn't like …	I apologise for …	Yours faithfully,
Bye!	Have fun!	Dear Madam,

D Write one or more of these compositions in formal style, using about 100 words. Look at the study box and the Ten Writing Tips on page 127 before you start.

1 You ordered a set of 200 sheets of writing paper with your name and address on, but when it arrived, you saw that they had spelt your name wrong. You complain and send it back. In your letter, ask them to correct the spelling and send you a new set of 200 sheets.

2 You have never met your father's boss, Mr Sunderland, but as you are the same age as his son Jack, he invited you to Jack's eighteenth birthday party. Unfortunately, on the day you completely forgot about it and did not go. Write to Mr Sunderland, apologising and saying you will be sending a small present to his son.

3 Look at this advertisement and write to apply for the job.

Can you teach canoeing?

Do you want to spend this summer in a beautiful part
of the world?

Then come and work with YLG!

We need canoeing experts to train beginners aged 14-20 at our sites
in the South of France from mid-July to the end of August.

You'll make friends, get a suntan and earn some money
at the same time!

Write to Young Leisure Group,
P.O. Box 473, Chichester PO19 3NB.

Informal letters

Make your **informal letters** relaxed and conversational. You can use **short forms**, lots of **questions**, and **exclamations**. Try to show you are really interested in what you are writing about.

Dear (name),

I'm sorry I haven't been in touch / written sooner.

I've been meaning to write for ages.

How are you? How's your family?

What's your new flat / job / boss like?

Guess what happened to me last week!

I'm having a dinner party on ...

It'd be really nice to see you again.

Do let me know if you can come.

All the best to your parents.

Looking forward to hearing from you soon.

We must get together soon.

Yours, / Regards, / Best wishes, / Love, / Love from ...

Sample task

You are writing a letter to your English penfriend, telling her about your recent trip to London. Write a letter of about 100 words in informal style. Do not include addresses.

Dear Nicola,

How are you? I hope everything's all right with you and your family. Are you still enjoying horse-riding? Have you fallen off yet?!

I'm writing to tell you about my trip to London. It was very exciting. Twenty of my classmates and I were on an exchange with a class from a north London school. I stayed with a very nice girl called Tracy. She likes playing tennis, too, so we played almost every day after school.

I think I learnt a lot of English!

Looking forward to hearing from you soon.

Love from

Gabriela

A Put the parts of this informal letter in the right order.

a Love, Margarita

b How are you these days?

c I'm writing because I want to invite you to a party.

d Please let me know as soon as possible.

e Do you think you can come?

f Dear Anita,

g I do hope you can.

h I hope you are enjoying your new job.

i It'll be on 27th June, from 8 p.m., at my flat.

j Hope to see you then.

B Complete the informal letter, using the expressions in the box.

How about	if you like	Best wishes	Isn't it fantastic
let me know	How are you	I'm sorry	Do you remember
It's really nice	I don't know why	guess what	for ages
		happened	

Dear Matt,

Are you surprised to hear from me? 1) _____ I haven't written for so long, but I've been very busy. 2) _____ ? I hope you're OK now, after your accident.

Well, 3) _____ to me last week! I got a new job! 4) _____ , I told you a long time ago that I had an interview with Microsoft in Seattle? I didn't get that job – 5) _____ . Perhaps they just didn't like me. But last Thursday I had an interview with IBM in Bristol, and I'm starting work there on Monday! 6) _____ !

I've found a flat already. 7) _____ , and it's in the city centre. You can come and stay, 8) _____ . 9) _____ one weekend soon? We haven't seen each other 10) _____ . Give me a ring to 11) _____ .

12) _____ ,

Steve

C Write one or both of these letters in informal style, using about 100 words. Look at the study box and the Ten Writing Tips on page 127 before you start.

1 Write a letter to a close friend, telling him / her about the terrible day you had last week, when lots of things went wrong. Here is your diary for that day:

Monday 8th April

Woke up late, because stayed up late last night watching horror film! Didn't have time for breakfast, so didn't feel right all day. Rushed off to school. In the hurry forgot to take my homework, so teacher was cross. Saw Tommy in the coffee break, but he didn't speak to me. I don't think he likes me any more!

Lunch was horrible – dry sandwich and apple. So bought some chocolate on the way home. Now will get fat!

At home Dad got angry with me, because he says I don't help Mum enough. Forgot to take the dog for walk. So had to do all the washing-up after supper. <u>And</u> two hours of homework to do! <u>And</u> nothing worth watching on TV! What a day!

2 This is part of a letter you receive from your new Australian penfriend, Felicity.

Hi there! I live in Brisbane, Queensland, and I have three sisters and a brother. We all love playing tennis. My favourite subject at school is history. What about you?

Now write a letter to Felicity, telling her about your family, your interests and where you live.

Descriptions of people, places and objects

Describing people
Practise using these words.
Remember – use paragraphs.

Hair	Shape	Character	Features
		Positive	
dark	tall	kind	beard
fair	short	polite	moustache
blonde	large	generous	fringe
grey	small	friendly	scar
long	fat	sociable	spots
short	thin		freckles
straight	plump	*Negative*	wrinkles
curly	slim	selfish	
wavy		rude	
spiky		mean	
bald		shy	

He always looks smart.   She wears lovely clothes.   He has a suntan.
She walks with a stick.   He's going bald.   She's a very kind person.
She usually wears glasses.   He's quite attractive / good-looking.
She has a small nose.   She looks like a film star!

(See **Unit 39** for clothes vocabulary.)

Sample task
Describe your best friend, using about 100 words.

My best friend is called Lydia. She lives in the house opposite, and goes to my school, so we see each other every day.

She is much **shorter** than me, and rather **plump**, because she loves eating! She has **long dark wavy hair**, and she **usually wears glasses**. In the summer she always **has a suntan**. At weekends she **wears smart clothes**, when we go to the cinema together.

She's my best friend because she's the nicest person I know. She's very **kind** and **generous**. My parents say she is very **polite**, too. I hope we'll always be friends.

A Write a description of one or more of these people, using about 100 words.

1 your best friend

2 an older person you admire and respect

3 your favourite singer, musician or actor

4 one of your neighbours

5 one of your teachers

6 your parents, brother or sister

Describing places
Practise using these words and phrases. **Remember** – use paragraphs.

village   town   city   capital   resort   the suburbs   gardens
offices   restaurants   shops   nightlife

Opposites: quiet ~ lively   boring ~ interesting   large ~ small
clean ~ dirty   cheap ~ expensive   beautiful ~ ugly   old ~ modern

(See **Unit 46** for scenery vocabulary.)

Sample task
Where do you live? Describe your city / town / village, using about 100 words.

I live in a **beautiful village** in Devon in the south-west of England. The houses are all very **old**, and they have lovely **gardens**. There is a church, a **small** supermarket, a pub, a fish-and-chip shop, and a post office. We go by bus to a nearby **town** to buy other things.

Because I've lived here all my life, I know everybody and they know me. Sometimes I feel the village is too **quiet**. It would be nice to meet more people! There is no **nightlife** for young people at all. But on the whole I'm happy here.

B Write one of these compositions using about 100 words.

1 Describe your town or village.
2 What would be your ideal place to live? Think about working or studying, shopping, spare time activities and transport.

Describing objects
Practise using these words and phrases. **Remember** – use paragraphs.

Size	Shape	Material	Colour	Pattern	
big	long	plastic	pale	plain	heavy
large	short	wood	dark	patterned	light
huge	thick	metal	red	with stripes /	hard
small	thin	gold	blue	striped	soft
tiny	square	silver	green	checked	rough
	rectangular	leather	yellow		smooth
	round	silk	pink		sharp
	diamond-		brown		
	shaped		grey		

a beautiful old house   an Italian silk scarf
an expensive designer jacket   a heavy leather suitcase

It's for opening bottles.   You can clean floors with it.
It's made of plastic.   It helps to keep you dry.

Sample task
Describe your pen, using about 50 words.

It's a **long thin** shape, and feels quite **light**. It's made of **metal** and **hard plastic**, and has a button you press when you want to write. The metal part looks like **silver**, and it has 'Parker' written round it. It writes very smoothly and well.

C Practise describing objects to a friend, who should try to guess what they are.

1 the most useful object in your daily life (something small like a toothbrush)
2 the most useful object in your kitchen at home (it could be small, like a potato peeler, or large, like a dishwasher)
3 the most useful piece of equipment in an office

D Write one or both of these compositions, using about 100 words.

1 Which three objects would you save from your house if it were on fire? Describe them and explain why they are important to you.
2 Have you got a lucky mascot, an object that you take everywhere with you, to bring you luck? If so, describe it and explain how you think it has helped you.

Telling a story

We usually use the **past continuous** to describe or set the scene:
- *It was raining as we ...*   • *People were talking when I ...*

the **past perfect** for flashbacks and earlier action:
- *I had been there before.*   • *I realised he hadn't seen me.*

and the **past simple** for action in the story:
- *We climbed to the top.*   • *They rushed inside.*   • *Just then the police arrived.*

You need to make a **plan**, and put your ideas into **paragraphs**, like this:
Paragraph 1 – describing the scene, with some flashbacks
Paragraph 2 – action
Paragraph 3 – more action, with a good final sentence

Final sentences
- *It was a(n) exciting / wonderful / memorable day for us.*   • *I really enjoyed my trip.*
- *It was the best / worst holiday I had ever had.*   • *Luckily, nobody was badly hurt.*
- *Eventually we all arrived home, tired but happy.*

Sample task
Your English teacher has asked you to write a story. It must begin with this sentence:
Suddenly a man pushed past me and ran out of the shop.
Write your story in about 100 words.

Suddenly a man pushed past me and ran out of the shop. I was buying some CDs at the time. I saw him jump into a car and drive off at top speed. I thought I recognised him – he used to live next door to me. Just then the police arrived. 'Did anyone see that man? He's an escaped prisoner!' they shouted.

They didn't catch him immediately, but I gave a description of him, which helped them to arrest him later. He's safely back in prison now. It was a very exciting afternoon for me!

A The past simple is the most common tense in a written story. Complete the sentences with the correct form of the past simple. Check the irregular verbs on page 128 if you aren't sure.

1 We _____ the photos yesterday. (take)
2 He _____ us all to Granada. (drive)
3 She _____ the lecture. (understand)
4 They _____ us some advice. (give)
5 He _____ the secret well. (keep)
6 I _____ up early. (wake)
7 She _____ round the bay. (swim)
8 They _____ their house last year. (sell)
9 He _____ home on his bike. (ride)
10 We _____ a UFO in the sky. (see)
11 The ship _____ that night. (sink)
12 I _____ him everything I _____ . (teach, know)
13 They _____ hands when they _____ . (shake, meet)
14 They _____ in love at first sight. (fall)
15 I _____ to ring her back. (forget)

16 We _____ by public transport. (go)

17 He _____ all his money. (lose)

18 They _____ a lot of mistakes. (make)

19 She _____ a different colour. (choose)

20 He _____ a millionaire. (become)

B Put the parts of this story in the right order.

a We had never camped before,

b Then it was time for supper –

c At first it was difficult to put the tents up,

d After doing the washing-up, we sat round the fire,

e It was a wonderful end to a perfect day.

f so that took us a long time.

g The sun was shining as we reached the campsite.

h talking, singing and telling stories.

i a delicious barbecue.

j but we were looking forward to the outdoor life.

C Complete the story, using the words in the box.

> as soon as   unfortunately   at last   before
> suddenly   after   then   as

Norman was fast asleep, dreaming happily about football, when
1) _____ his alarm clock rang very loudly, right in his ear.
2) _____ he heard it, he jumped out of bed and started to
get dressed. 'Quick, quick, I mustn't be late for school again!' he thought.
He threw some water over his face, 3) _____ rushed downstairs.
4) _____ , there was no time for him to have breakfast
5) _____ leaving the house. He'd be hungry by lunchtime,
6) _____ he had no money to buy any drinks or snacks.
7) _____ waiting a long time at the bus stop, he finally caught the
bus, and 8) _____ he arrived at school. He couldn't believe his
eyes – the gates were shut. It was Saturday – no school that day!

D The editor of an English magazine has asked you to write a story, which may be published in the magazine. Choose one or more of these titles, and write your story in about 100 words. Look at the study box and the Ten Writing Tips on page 127 before you start.

> **An interesting visit**
> **An accident**
> **The funniest thing that has ever happened to me**
> **The best / worst holiday I have ever had**

UNIT 87

Writing a diary

You can choose your own personal style for writing a diary, but most diaries are written in **short sentences**, sometimes almost in **note form**. Diary language is **conversational**, with short forms (*I'll, don't, can't*) and exclamations (*!*), and very often no subject pronoun or articles (*I, he, she, the, a, an*):
• *Forgot my door key today, so had to borrow neighbour's!*

Diary-writing is an excellent way of helping yourself to think in English. The best time to write it is in the evening, before you go to bed.

Topics for your diary
things that have happened to you (good or bad?)
exciting news you have received
people you have met (interesting or boring?)
things to remember for tomorrow
thoughts, feelings and impressions

Sample task
Write a diary page for one day of your most recent holidays. Write about 100 words, in conversational style.

Arrived in Madrid early afternoon. Checked into hotel in city centre. Had a shower (terribly hot here!) and put on light clothes. Out to the Prado (wonderful paintings but very crowded) and then coffee outside, in Retiro Park. Back to hotel for short 'siesta' (that's what people do here!), and then out again to meet Paloma and Carmen. Took us on tour of five or six bars, eating delicious little snacks ('tapas') in each one. By midnight, feeling *really* tired, but Paloma and Carmen said it was too early to sleep. Drove us all round Madrid, showing us famous buildings. It was fantastic, but didn't get back to hotel until 4 a.m.! Wow!

A Rewrite the sentences in a shorter form, as they might appear in a diary. Remember that you can usually remove subject pronouns and articles (and sometimes the verb *be*).

1 I went to Athens for an important meeting.
2 Pam forgot to close the back door, so the cat got in.
3 I arrived at the bank. It was closed, so I couldn't pay in the cheque.
4 Dimitri drove to the airport to meet his grandmother.
5 I hope our team will win the match.
6 Rita told me to apply for the job in the Export Department.
7 The book I wanted was not available.
8 It was a great party. I had a super time.
9 Remember to go to the library, and do the shopping, too.
10 I invited all my friends to the barbecue.

B Look at what happened to Lucia last week. She had a very busy time. What do you think she would write in her diary? Fill it in for her.

On Sunday she flew to Amsterdam to meet her friend Heidi. They went to lunch in a restaurant with some of Heidi's friends, as it was Lucia's birthday. Then Lucia stayed the night at Heidi's house.

On Monday she flew to Florence, to have a business meeting with the manager of a sportswear company in the afternoon. She stayed in a hotel, and went to bed early, because she was tired.

On Tuesday she went to the Uffizi art gallery in the morning, and then had lunch in a café. In the afternoon she flew back to London.

On Wednesday she was in the London office, writing reports and having meetings with her boss. She played tennis with Alex after work.

Then on Thursday she went to Oxford by train to see Mr Hansen, the manager of a factory that produces jeans. They went to a restaurant for lunch. Unfortunately, she dropped her door key somewhere in the restaurant, and so when she arrived back in London, she had to break a window to get into her flat.

On Friday she had a quiet day in the office, and watched television in the evening.

On Saturday she went shopping and bought two pairs of shoes. She invited three friends to dinner in the evening – Ted, Susie and Jeremy.

SUNDAY

MONDAY

TUESDAY

WEDNESDAY

THURSDAY

FRIDAY

SATURDAY

C Now write a diary page for one or more of these days. Try to make it as lively and interesting as possible.

1 your first day of a new language course (possibly in another country), or at a new school

2 a day when you had to take an important examination in your worst subject

3 a day when you were shocked or hurt by someone or something

4 a day when you had far too much work or studying to do

5 your last birthday

Correcting your writing

It is useful to be able to **correct your own mistakes**. Here are some ways of training yourself to do this:

Look at the homework your teacher has corrected, and **make a list of mistakes** you have made more than once. Keep this as a check list.

Practise looking for mistakes by **exchanging homework** with another student. Look for each other's mistakes.

Write the mistakes you often make, with the correct form, on pieces of paper and **stick them round your room** or in your notebook. Try to learn to recognise them and correct them next time.

Always make time to **check your writing before giving it in**. Use your check list to search for your mistakes, and look for new ones!

A Correct the mistakes in the letter.

Dear Rick,

It was so nice to get the letter of you. I want to write you a long time, but you now I'm very lazy!

I'm glad you enjoy you're new job. I think it's very funny, is it? Since I've saw you last time I am doing many diferent thing. First I traveled to rome to met my frend, then we went to south italy for picking the grapes. It was a hard work but the pay was well. After three month I back home to go on study at university. Now I'm looking forward for the holidays next year!

May you come to visit me? Their's lots of rooms for you to sleep on my floor! Right and tell me soon.

Goodbye,

Your freind Daniel

B There is at least one grammar mistake in each of the sentences. Find the mistakes and correct them.

1 I live near the city centre since I arrived Kyoto.
2 Andy is washing the dishes every evening after supper.
3 All the people in the office was working hardly that day.
4 We could go to cinema if there is good film on.
5 I think everybody like the new Italian restaurant.
6 Keith forgotten his umbrella, so he got wet.
7 Your hair looks great! Have you cut it yesterday?
8 The old man was wearing a very dirty trouser.
9 The police was very gratefully for the informations.
10 Fritz studied hard, but had failed the exam.
11 The television news were not very interested today.
12 Although raining, we went shopping anyway.

Ten Writing Tips

1 Keep your style **friendly and informal** in letters to friends. OK? Got that?
2 Make sure you use the **correct letter style**.
   (*Dear Sir or Madam, ... Lots and lots of love and kisses from Snoopy*)
3 **Make a plan**. Don't just write everything that comes into your head.
   Well, I think ... You see, ... This is a difficult question ... I'm not sure ...
4 **Watch out** four speling misstakes!
5 Don't **repeat** repeat repeat yourself yourself.
6 Don't use too many exclamation marks**!!!!!!!!!**
7 Should you use **questions** or short answers in formal letters? No, not usually.
8 Kindly make every effort to maintain **formality** in formal compositions.
9 When you've finished, **check** (control?) words you often confuse.
10 Have you **really** answered the question? Er ..., maybe, maybe not.

C Can you answer the questions on writing? Read **Units 78–88** carefully first.

1 **Spelling**
   A What is the plural of *man, child, tooth, foot, beach, leaf, tomato?*
   B Correct these words: *theif, runing, ponys, climing, nee, helpfull*

2 **Postcards**
   A Which style should you most often use?
   B What ending should you use if you don't know someone well?

3 **E-mails and notes**
   A Can you start an e-mail with *Hi* or *Hello?*
   B What should you put at the end of a note?

4 **Filling in forms**
   A Give some examples of *occupation.*
   B What four things could people write for *marital status?*

5 **Sentence building**
   A Which of these two words have a similar meaning?
      during   although   while
   B Which is correct – *such a big dog* or *so a big dog?*

6 **Letters**
   A What is the correct ending to a letter beginning *Dear Mrs Hall?*
   B Which is correct – *Dear friend* or *Dear James?*

7 **Descriptions of people**
   A Write down five words describing people's shapes.
   B Write down five words describing people's characters.

8 **Telling a story**
   A Which three tenses do you usually use?
   B Do you need a plan or not?

9 **Writing a diary**
   A How can writing a diary help with your English?
   B How is it different from other types of writing?

IRREGULAR VERBS

Infinitive	Past simple	Past participle	Infinitive	Past simple	Past participle
be	was/were	been	learn	learnt, learned	learnt, learned
beat	beat	beaten	leave	left	left
become	became	become	lend	lent	lent
begin	began	begun	let	let	let
bend	bent	bent	lie	lay	lain
bite	bit	bitten	lose	lost	lost
blow	blew	blown			
break	broke	broken	make	made	made
bring	brought	brought	mean	meant	meant
build	built	built	meet	met	met
burn	burnt, burned	burnt, burned			
buy	bought	bought	pay	paid	paid
			put	put	put
catch	caught	caught			
choose	chose	chosen	read	read	read
come	came	come	ride	rode	ridden
cost	cost	cost	ring	rang	rung
cut	cut	cut	rise	rose	risen
			run	ran	run
do	did	done			
draw	drew	drawn	say	said	said
dream	dreamt, dreamed	dreamt, dreamed	see	saw	seen
drink	drank	drunk	sell	sold	sold
drive	drove	driven	send	sent	sent
			shake	shook	shaken
eat	ate	eaten	shine	shone	shone
			shoot	shot	shot
fall	fell	fallen	show	showed	shown, showed
feed	fed	fed	shut	shut	shut
feel	felt	felt	sing	sang	sung
fight	fought	fought	sink	sank	sunk
find	found	found	sit	sat	sat
fly	flew	flown	sleep	slept	slept
forget	forgot	forgotten	smell	smelt, smelled	smelt, smelled
freeze	froze	frozen	speak	spoke	spoken
			spend	spent	spent
get	got	got	stand	stood	stood
give	gave	given	steal	stole	stolen
go	went	gone	stick	stuck	stuck
grow	grew	grown	strike	struck	struck
			swim	swam	swum
hang	hung	hung			
have	had	had	take	took	taken
hear	heard	heard	teach	taught	taught
hide	hid	hidden	tear	tore	torn
hit	hit	hit	tell	told	told
hold	held	held	think	thought	thought
hurt	hurt	hurt	throw	threw	thrown
keep	kept	kept	understand	understood	understood
know	knew	known			
			wake	woke	woken
lay	laid	laid	wear	wore	worn
lead	led	led	win	won	won
lean	leant, leaned	leant, leaned	write	wrote	written

Unit 1

A
1	rises	6	teaches
2	tells	7	drives
3	close	8	phones
4	comes	9	help
5	makes	10	drink

B
1 Where does Miho come from?
2 When do you listen to BBC World Service?
3 Why do you sometimes lend James money?
4 Who speaks Spanish?
5 Does he pay his bills every three months?
6 Do your friends agree with you?
7 Do his friends and relatives send him cards on his birthday?
8 Do I/you need to see the dentist twice a year?

C
1 I don't work for a large company.
2 Pierre doesn't write to his parents every week.
3 We don't often eat chocolate in the evening.
4 The old man doesn't always swim in the sea before lunch.
5 We don't believe what you say.
6 Daisy doesn't often ride her bike these days.

Unit 2

A
1 is having
2 is freezing
3 is reading
4 is driving
5 is wearing
6 are losing
7 isn't eating, is just drinking
8 is hurrying
9 is showing
10 is studying

B
1 are you staying
2 are you planning
3 are you doing
4 are you hoping
5 are you going

C
1 I don't understand what the teacher said.
2 Does this dictionary belong to you?
3 ✔
4 What does this word mean, please?
5 I need a lot more information before I decide.
6 ✔
7 ✔
8 How much do you know about your family history?

Unit 3

A
1	There's	4	it's
2	It's	5	there's
3	Is there	6	is it

B
1	they're	4	Are there
2	there are	5	they're
3	there are	6	are they

C *It's:* 1, 5, 6, 9, 10, 11, 13, 15
There's: 2, 3, 4, 7, 8, 12, 14, 16

Unit 4

A
1 will be
2 does the overnight coach depart
3 Shall we put
4 is going to save
5 am visiting/am going to visit
6 Will you come
7 will never do
8 'll answer

B 1E 2J 3A 4I 5B 6D
7C 8G 9F 10H

C
1 What are you doing this weekend?
2 How long does/will the journey from Milan to Brussels take?
3 What will you do/are you going to do when you leave school?
4 Shall I help you with all that work?
5 When does the Stuttgart train arrive?
6 Shall I shut the door before we start the meeting?
7 Who are you taking/going to take to the party on Saturday?
8 Do you think she'll win the match?
9 Will you marry me?
10 Shall we order some coffee before we get the bill?
11 Why aren't you going on holiday to the Canaries again this year?
12 If there's enough time, will you ask him to explain?
13 I'll close the window.
14 I'll catch you if you fall!
15 No, but I'm seeing/going to see it this evening.

D *What are you doing on Monday?*
I'm going to the dentist at 10 (in the morning). I'm having/going to a Spanish conversation class at 11. I'm going for/having a swim at 12.30. In the afternoon I'm studying/going to study for my Economics exam at home.

What are you doing on Tuesday?
I'm having/going to an Economics lecture in Room 12 at 11. I'm meeting/going to meet Elaine for lunch at the sandwich bar at 12.30. I'm working/going to work in the self-study centre from 4 to 6. I'm going to Manuel's for supper at 8 (in the evening).

What are you doing on Wednesday?
I'm going to Spanish classes in Room 21 from 9 to 11 (in the morning). I'm having/going to have my hair cut at Split Ends at 12. I'm going to a keep-fit class at 3. I'm meeting/going to meet Ali at the Odeon cinema at 7.30 (in the evening).

What are you doing on Thursday?
(In the morning) I'm studying/going to study in the university library from 9 to 12. Then I'm going to an Economics lecture in Room 6 at 2 (o'clock). I'm having/going to a Spanish lecture in Room 43 at 4 (in the afternoon). I'm going to Darren's to study Economics with him at 8 (in the evening).

What are you doing on Friday?
I'm taking/going to take an Economics exam in the Lecture Hall from 9 to 12. Then I'm meeting/going to meet the whole class for lunch at Roberto's Pizza House. I'm going to football team practice from 3 to 5 (in the afternoon). I'm meeting/going to meet Charles and Dora at the Café Rouge at 7.30.

What are you doing on Saturday?
In the morning I'm doing/going to do the supermarket shopping. I'm playing/going to play in a football match at 2 (in the afternoon). I'm going to the Students' Disco at 7 (in the evening).

What are you doing on Sunday?
I'm getting/going to get up late! In the morning I'm going for a long walk with Elaine. I'm having/going to have lunch at Ali's house at 1 (o'clock). In the afternoon I'm doing/going to do my Spanish homework. I'm discussing/going to discuss holiday plans with Elaine, Manuel and Charles at 8 (in the evening).

Unit 5

A 1 plays
2 do you usually get up
3 do you speak
4 wears
5 doesn't take
6 does this sentence mean
7 lives
8 works

9 seems
10 don't belong
11 washes
12 Does your brother cook, says, does

B 1E 2I 3A 4J 5B 6H
7C 8D 9F 10G

C 1 I'm writing a letter at the moment.
2 He washes his car every Sunday afternoon.
3 ✔
4 ✔
5 ✔
6 Look, the plane is taking off.
7 He's Swiss and he comes from Berne.
8 I'm going to borrow a video and watch it.
9 Do you own a house or a flat?
10 Shall I carry it for you?
11 I believe every word you say.
12 I promise I'll do my best tomorrow.

D 1C 2D 3A 4B 5F 6E

E 1 contains
2 going to
3 a difficult problem
4 come to lunch
5 goes
6 this word mean
7 arrive in
8 I'll finish/to finish
9 does he
10 doesn't belong

F 1 doesn't   6 aren't
2 isn't   7 are
3 do   8 Shall
4 can't   9 was
5 Don't   10 going

Unit 6

A 1I 2G 3A 4H 5C 6B
7D 8F 9J 10E

B 1 These people are always very kind and helpful.
2 ✔
3 I can't read any of these books – they're so boring/any of this book – it's so boring.

4 All these cars are parked in the wrong place.
5 ✔
6 How many of these exercises did you get right?
7 Those are the students who were in my class.
8 ✔
9 Stop making all this noise at once!
10 Where did you get all that money from?

C 1 This   6 this
2 that/this   7 those
3 those   8 these
4 that   9 that
5 that   10 this

D 1 yourselves   4 myself
2 yourself   5 ourselves
3 himself   6 herself

E his his himself, her hers herself, its – itself, our ours ourselves, your yours yourself/yourselves, their theirs themselves

Unit 7

A 1 bought   6 taught
2 took   7 cost
3 bit   8 slept
4 wrote   9 forgot
5 drove   10 made

B 1 didn't build
2 Did you leave
3 didn't go
4 broke
5 threw
6 didn't steal
7 Did your horse win
8 didn't catch
9 didn't lose
10 Did the robbers hide
11 gave
12 didn't spend

C 1 were   9 got up
2 came   10 couldn't
3 realised   11 fell
4 broke   12 knew
5 had to   13 arrived
6 put   14 said
7 hit   15 returned
8 heard   16 thought

D *Possible questions:*

1 Where does/did Uncle Bob come from/live?
2 What did he break?
3 Where did the golf ball hit him?
4 How often/How many times did he go to hospital/see the same doctor?
5 Why did he return/go back to Australia.

E 1 Did   4 Did
   2 Was   5 Did
   3 Were   6 Were

Unit 8

A 1 was walking
2 was talking
3 was she doing
4 were watching
5 was living
6 were waiting
7 was washing
8 Were you driving

B 1 was shining
2 was feeling
3 were singing
4 was getting
5 was beginning

C 1 was talking   3 ran
   2 were playing   4 helped

D 1 had passed (*1st action: passing her exams*)
2 had been (*1st action: being there before*)
3 had already seen (*1st action: seeing the film*)
4 had never lived (*1st action: not living alone*)
5 hadn't seen (*1st action: not sending the letters*)
6 hadn't (ever) met (*1st action: not meeting her*)
7 had already put out (*1st action: putting out the fire*)
8 had never worked (*1st action: working in a call centre*)

E 1D (*1st action: a friend recommending the hotel*)
2A (*1st action: forgetting to put a stamp on it*)

3E (*1st action: not eating snails*)
4B (*1st action: the guests leaving*)
5C (*1st action: managing to start the car*)

F 1 We finished our lunch and *left* the restaurant soon afterwards.
2 When Clive passed his driving test, his father *bought* him a car.
3 ✔   4 ✔   5 ✔

Unit 9

A 1 I haven't written to him often enough.
2 Has Penny switched off the television yet?
3 They have nearly finished their work, and it's only lunch-time!
4 He's saved a lot of money since January.
5 Have you ever seen a flying fish?
6 Have you seen any good films lately?
7 We really haven't made much progress so far.
8 I've already done the shopping.

B 1 for   5 for
   2 since   6 since
   3 Since   7 for
   4 for   8 since

C 1 We haven't seen Fred for a long time.
2 She has gone to the post office.
3 Susan has not moved into her new flat yet.
4 My cat has just had kittens.
5 I've already paid the bill.
6 He has planted a new fruit tree in his garden.
7 The engineers have started the work now.
8 She has only just come back from her holiday.

D 1 I bought the car last year.
2 ✔
3 ✔

4 I've been here since January 1st.
5 They've never eaten fish and chips before.
6 ✔
7 My friends have already studied English for ten years.
8 That was a great film we saw last night.

E 1 has been studying, since
2 have been waiting, for
3 have been saving up, since
4 have been typing, for
5 has been going, for
6 have been working, since
7 For, have been living
8 since, has been learning

F 1 won
2 didn't hear
3 have you been doing
4 Have you bought
5 learnt
6 forgot
7 Have you ever been
8 Were you interested
9 have you studied/have you been studying
10 has just passed
11 bought
12 have lost
13 moved
14 Did you sleep
15 have made/have been making

Unit 10

A 1 was
2 felt/was feeling
3 could not
4 looked
5 noticed
6 wasn't
7 said
8 got up
9 opened
10 saw
11 started
12 found
13 were
14 were moving
15 heard

16 began/was beginning
17 came
18 told
19 Have you come
20 didn't like
21 didn't want
22 tried
23 didn't move
24 came
25 said
26 shouted
27 put
28 repeated
29 woke up
30 was
31 was shaking
32 was saying/said
33 thought

B 1E 2A 3F 4B 5G 6C
7J 8D 9H 10I

C 1B 2C 3A 4D 5A 6C
7B 8A 9D 10B 11C
12A 13B 14C

D 1 went to Portugal
2 you been doing
3 the car repaired
4 never been
5 theirs
6 had seen/met him
7 the robber had
8 been
9 you had/owned
10 having (my) breakfast

Unit 11
A 1 an 7 an
2 the 8 the
3 – 9 the
4 – 10 a
5 – 11 the
6 an 12 a

B 1 the cinema
2 a moment
3 (the) time
4 France
5 tennis
6 music
7 the office
8 a problem
9 the phone
10 North Street

Unit 12
A 1D 2I 3E 4G 5B 6F
7C 8A 9J 10H

B 1 mustn't 4 ought
2 may 5 Can/May
3 should

Unit 13
A 1 Where 6 What
2 How long 7 Who
3 What, What 8 What, How
4 Where 9 Which
5 What 10 What

B 1 Whose is this watch?
2 How long have you been studying/learning English?
3 Why is this exercise wrong?
4 Who was at the disco?
5 How does the heating/air-conditioning work?
6 How much was your bag?
7 When did you do your homework?
8 Where are you/we going on holiday next year?
9 Why did you do that?
10 What is that book called?

C 1 where C 4 who B
2 why E 5 which D
3 whose A

D 1 who 6 where
2 who 7 where
3 which 8 what
4 who 9 who
5 why 10 whose

Unit 14
A *Countable:* tomato, student, vegetables, people, rooms, shoe, book, car.
The rest are uncountable.

B 1 only a little information
2 not much wine
3 only a few tomatoes
4 not much bread
5 not many people
6 only a little money
7 not many cars
8 only a little advice

C 1C 2J 3A 4G 5B 6D
7E 8F 9H 10I

Unit 15
A 1 a
2 who
3 home
4 before
5 had
6 herself
7 some
8 her
9 carefully
10 a
11 there
12 back/home
13 saw/noticed/realized
14 had
15 little
16 who
17 thought/said
18 put/left
19 had/were
20 MINE

B 1 any tea
2 a lot of cassettes
3 some cream
4 any paper
5 a little advice
6 a few people
7 much work
8 some money
9 many flowers
10 any news
11 some information
12 any of the music
13 Some students
14 a few more sandwiches
15 much idea

C 1 the Town Hall
2 Literature
3 the flute
4 home
5 green tea
6 ice hockey
7 love
8 Bulgaria
9 Raw fish
10 big dogs

D 1 ought to/should see
2 mustn't/can't smoke
3 can speak
4 whose brother won
5 you going to

6 can't come
7 does this word
8 must/should/ought to keep
9 since
10 may I
11 took/stole
12 were having

Unit 16

A 1 Biscuits are made in that factory.
2 The secret agent was arrested at Zurich airport last week.
3 The key is kept in that box.
4 Hazel was taught by Miss Jones last year, I think.
5 The grass is always cut every week.
6 Were you given the right information yesterday?
7 You weren't invited to the party a fortnight ago.
8 Was the stolen car ever found?/Has the stolen car ever been found?

B 1 was given
2 weren't locked
3 was eaten
4 is spoken
5 are usually checked
6 was seen
7 is exported
8 was badly hurt

C 1F 2E 3A 4C 5B 6D

Unit 17

A 1 to   5 to   9 to   13 to
2 at   6 in   10 at   14 in
3 on   7 at   11 at
4 in   8 in   12 on

B 1 under   4 Beside
2 near   5 in front of
3 Behind   6 under

C 1 on   8 in (the)   15 at
2 in   9 on   16 in
3 at   10 in   17 at
4 at   11 at   18 on
5 on   12 on   19 at
6 on   13 in (the)   20 in
7 on   14 on   21 at

Unit 18

A 1 if D   6 if E
2 if H   7 if C
3 if A   8 if G
4 unless J   9 unless B
5 if I   10 unless F

B *Suggested answers:*
1 I'll ask someone to help me
2 I'll read a good book instead
3 I'll certainly accept
4 we'll get a taxi
5 I'll suggest Fiji
6 I'll be delighted
7 If I win the race
8 If anybody asks what I want for my birthday
9 If you invite me to dinner
10 If I fail my exams
11 If I get fat
12 If the Prime Minister offers me a place in his government

C 1 told, 'd believe
2 could, let
3 were, 'd buy
4 went, 'd get
5 went, 'd cost

D *Suggested answers:*
1 I'd put it out.
2 I'd call an ambulance.
3 I'd give him some small change.
4 I'd pay on the train.
5 I'd ask them to wait, and rush home for my money.

E 1 I'd be
2 I'd visit
3 spoke Arabic
4 were you
5 became rich

F *Suggested answers:*
If I were you, ...
1 I'd take an aspirin.
2 I'd ring up the credit card company.
3 I'd tell her.
4 I wouldn't watch so much television/I'd watch less television.
5 I'd tell my father everything.

6 I'd start studying now.
7 I'd take some exercise.
8 I'd think again!

Unit 19

A 1 more difficult
2 cleverer
3 more comfortable
4 easier
5 better
6 happier
7 further/farther
8 bigger
9 worse
10 more helpful
11 darker
12 more convenient
13 more beautiful
14 more intelligent
15 untidier
16 redder
17 more modern
18 uglier
19 more delicious
20 sunnier

B 1 My room isn't as untidy as yours.
2 Your teacher isn't as helpful as mine.
3 Living in a village isn't as much fun as living in a town.
4 Biscuits aren't as good for your health as fresh fruit.
5 A bike isn't as convenient in the rain as a car.
6 English isn't as difficult to learn as Chinese.
7 A cake isn't as easy to cook as an omelette.
8 Josie isn't as good at meeting people as Giorgio.

2 My teacher is more helpful than yours.
3 Living in a town is more fun than living in a village.
4 Fresh fruit is better for your health than biscuits.
5 A car is more convenient in the rain than a bike.
6 Chinese is more difficult to learn than English.
7 An omelette is easier to cook than a cake.

8 Giorgio is better at meeting people than Josie.

C 1 more 4 lighter
2 than 5 better
3 cheaper 6 as

D 1 the best
2 the fattest
3 the happiest
4 the youngest
5 the most difficult
6 the richest
7 the most useful
8 the worst
9 the ugliest
10 the longest
11 the furthest/farthest
12 the most comfortable
13 the widest
14 the thinnest
15 the most romantic
16 the tidiest
17 the strongest
18 the prettiest
19 the whitest
20 the fastest

E 1 the highest
2 the longest
3 the biggest
4 the most successful
5 the largest, (the) deepest
6 the largest
7 the smallest
8 the fastest
9 the longest
10 the highest
11 the largest, the oldest
12 the most popular
13 the best
14 the worst
15 the easiest

Unit 20

A 1 from
2 at, in, at
3 to, to
4 near, at
5 at, at, in
6 by, at
7 in, in
8 on, in
9 by
10 to, to, for, for

11 in, near
12 at, in, From, to
13 on, at, in, on
14 On, to, on, to
15 at, in, on, at
16 in (the), in (the)
17 in, in, on
18 near, in

B 1 take as long
2 was given
3 I'd be
4 further/farther (away) from
5 hasn't flown
6 taller than she
7 were found
8 drink as much

C 1G 2I 3F 4H 5A 6B
7J 8C 9E 10D

D 1 a 7 been
2 on 8 for
3 gave 9 put/arranged
4 is 10 at
5 than 11 myself
6 lot 12 better

Unit 21

A 1 borrow 5 lend
2 Come 6 bring
3 used 7 used
4 take 8 go

B 1A 2A 3B 4A 5A 6B

C 1 come, bring
2 lent
3 walk
4 Go, take
5 spending
6 take, go

Unit 22

A *Suggested answers:*
1 ADJ intelligent
2 ADJ funny
3 ADV slowly
4 ADJ large
5 ADV well
6 ADV beautifully
7 ADV Suddenly
8 ADV awfully
9 ADJ antique
10 ADV kindly

B 1 thrilled 4 boring
2 amusing 5 fascinating
3 interested

C 1 quietly 4 honest
2 fast 5 angrily
3 delicious

Unit 23

A 1 Suddenly we heard a crash.
2 She likes strawberries and cream very much.
3 We sometimes go shopping in the afternoon.
4 I think he washes his hair twice a week.
5 We have often seen him waiting at the bus stop.
6 Every day we go to school./We go to school every day.
7 I'm hoping to get a letter tomorrow./ Tomorrow I'm hoping to get a letter.
8 She usually takes her dog for a walk after breakfast.
9 He walked down the street very slowly.
10 Could you ask him to come as soon as possible?
11 He accepted the job immediately.
12 She never drinks coffee in the evening.
13 We had to learn the grammar rules by heart.
14 Last year nobody studied hard enough./Nobody studied hard enough last year.
15 I have seldom eaten such tasty rice.

B 1 We sometimes go to the theatre in Frankfurt.
2 The children behaved extremely well.
3 She likes walking in the rain very much.
4 Every day Adam does his homework./Adam does his homework every day.
5 They have never been to Cairo.
6 Do you often jog round the park?

7 I sent him a postcard yesterday.

8 Will they be there on time?

9 He has never driven her new car.

10 Do you often have headaches?

11 He spoke to me extremely kindly.

12 Suddenly the police car arrived on the scene.

13 Last week they bought a new computer./They bought a new computer last week.

14 He sat down happily to eat his supper.

C 1Ga 2Ae 3Hc 4Bb 5Df 6Cg 7Fd 8Eh

D
1 still
2 hardly
3 yet, already
4 still
5 hardly
6 already
7 yet
8 still
9 hardly
10 already
11 still
12 yet

Unit 24

A
1 watching
2 Taking
3 repairing
4 typing
5 walking
6 helping

B
1 to buy
2 give
3 go
4 reply
5 to visit
6 join
7 finish
8 to get

C 1G 2I 3A 4F 5B 6D 7H 8E 9C

Unit 25

A 1C 2A 3D 4A 5B 6A 7C 8D 9B 10A

B 1B 2G 3D 4A 5F 6A 7F 8E 9G 10B 11A 12A 13B 14C 15B

C
1 lend
2 angrily
3 still
4 bring
5 hard
6 hitting
7 getting
8 often

D
1 expensive (for us)
2 really delicious
3 speak (any)
4 should send him
5 tall enough to
6 very well

7 to come
8 fascinating
9 stay at home/in
10 (very) often
11 I'd like
12 as easy as
13 won
14 was arrested
15 I'll apply/ I might apply

Unit 26

A 1C 2F 3D 4E 5H 6G 7A 8B

B I think you should have .../ Why don't you have ...
1 it painted/decorated
2 it cut
3 it coloured/restyled/dyed
4 them cleaned
5 it repaired/mended/ fixed/serviced
6 a dress made
7 central heating installed/ put in
8 it serviced/checked
9 it repaired/mended
10 it tuned
11 it cleaned
12 it mended/repaired/fixed

Unit 27

A He said (that) .../He told me (that) ...
1 his name was Pablo.
2 he lived in Austria.
3 he had a brother and a sister.
4 his father was a manager.
5 his mother worked in a bank.
6 he was a very sociable person.
7 he liked pop music.
8 his best subject was history.
9 he walked to school every day.
10 he could swim very fast.

B 1 Sarah said (that) she would be there by 2 o'clock.
2 Michael said (that) Tony always worked very hard.

3 Patrick said (that) he thought (that) she ate too much chocolate.

4 The two men said (that) they would help us if they could.

5 Betty said (that) she didn't feel very well.

6 Liz said (that) she was going to the dentist the next day.

7 Anna said (that) she was sure (that) she could finish it in time.

8 The teacher said (that) we had all done very well in the test.

C
1 the students to
2 not to park
3 to help her
4 to buy/get some
5 not to phone
6 to get/fetch it
7 to give it
8 to give it

D 1J 2E 3A 4F 5B 6D 7I 8G 9H 10C

Unit 28

A
1 find out   5 take off
2 look after 6 turn on
3 look, up   7 call for
4 sort, out   8 give up

B 1E 2H 3A 4C 5B 6J 7D 8I 9G 10F

Unit 29

A
1 while
2 (in order) to
3 because
4 so, that
5 either, or
6 such, that, when
7 Although
8 to, but

B 1G 2H 3E 4A 5B 6F 7C 8D

Unit 30

A 1A 2C 3B 4D 5B 6C 7B 8A 9D 10A 11C 12B

B 1D 2G 3H 4I 5B 6A 7C 8F 9J 10E

KEY

C 1 Although 6 so
2 after 7 to
3 because 8 since
4 so that 9 as soon as
5 and 10 while

D 1 not to open
2 my hair restyled
3 out of coffee
4 she would do
5 getting on
6 for you
7 could see me
8 comes/is here soon
9 new kitchen fitted
10 off at
11 made by
12 had more/enough money

Unit 31

A 1 luck
2 friendships, education
3 improvement, anger
4 sense, humour, difficulties
5 surprise

B 1 relationship 6 reality
2 imagination 7 love
3 idea 8 neighbourhood
4 kindness 9 warmth
5 amazement 10 freedom

C 1 rock 7 car
2 dish 8 note
3 fish 9 tennis
4 dinner 10 strawberry
5 arm 11 helicopter
6 guard 12 computer

D 1 a stone floor
2 a television engineer
3 a bus driver
4 a road sign
5 a money belt
6 customer service
7 a town museum
8 a furniture shop
9 a vacuum cleaner
10 olive oil

E 1 men's shoes
2 the cat's milk
3 a girl's blue coat
4 her parents' house
5 a giraffe's neck
6 a letter of hers

7 painters' brushes
8 today's menu
9 people's ideas
10 a cook's knife
11 the doctor's advice
12 a story of yours
13 a child's cry
14 the Queen's palace
15 children's clothes
16 a bird's nest
17 Tuesday's meeting
18 the soldiers' uniforms
19 the students' success
20 a chef's hat

Unit 32

A 1H 2D 3A 4J 5E 6F
7B 8G 9I 10C

B 1 during 4 at
2 in, for 5 on
3 At, of 6 at

C 1 She soon became *bored with* her new job.
2 My friends and I travelled round the island *by motorbike/on our motorbikes*.
3 ✔
4 Duncan works in publishing, *like* my brother.
5 ✔
6 *At last* he's decided what to do.
7 I think Joanna is *related to* Madonna.
8 My laptop is *for sale*, if anyone's interested.
9 ✔
10 Perhaps I'll go – it *depends on* the weather.
11 Be careful – I think you're falling in love *with* him!
12 We *reached the hotel* in time for dinner.

Unit 33

A 1F 2A 3D 4B 5C 6E

B 1 That's a difficult situation – I think you *should* get some help.
2 *Could/Would/Can/Will* you show me how to use the photocopier, please?

3 You don't need *to* drive so fast – there's no hurry.
4 I'll *have to* take a taxi, if I want to get to the meeting on time.
5 We were angry because we *could* only answer half the questions in the test.
6 You don't *have to* do it, but it's a good idea.
7 If I were you *I* wouldn't leave school at sixteen.
8 Don't be unhappy! You *should/could* try and look on the bright side of life.
9 Harry *needn't do* this homework – he's already done more than the rest of you!
10 *Could/Would/Can/Will* you give me a hand with the sofa, please? I can't lift it.

Unit 34

A 1 My mother didn't want *me to* go to college.
2 The office manager let *me go* home early.
3 ✔
4 They don't *allow students* to use mobile phones in class.
5 ✔
6 ✔
7 We didn't *ask you to clean* our car.
8 ✔
9 The captain ordered *his men* to march on.
10 I'd prefer *you to book* a table for 7.30, not 8 p.m.

B 1 The postman handed me the letter.
2 I can lend you some money.
3 Can you send me the bill as soon as possible?
4 I taught him a useful bit of maths.
5 We bought him a really nice present.
6 I took her some flowers for her birthday.
7 Show it to me at once!
8 You can give it to them tomorrow.

Unit 35

A 1B 2D 3C 4D 5A 6C
7A 8D 9B 10B 11A
12C 13A 14D

B 1 should   6 you to
2 on   7 war
3 discuss   8 needn't
4 means   9 reached
5 it to me   10 friend

C 1 you to
2 have to/need to
3 me to borrow/use
4 ought to/should
5 freedom
6 children's
7 the cause of
8 married to
9 with
10 gave him

D 1 at, at
2 with, to, in, with
3 for, in, for
4 At, of, for
5 for, to, with
6 on, at
7 of, for
8 with, in
9 on
10 on/during, of

Unit 36

A 1 Swiss
2 Maltese
3 Dutch
4 Chinese
5 Iraqi
6 Icelandic
7 (North) American
8 Turkish
9 Greek
10 Portuguese
11 Danish
12 Thai
13 Welsh
14 Kuwaiti
15 Japanese

B 1 Polish/French
2 French
3 Spanish
4 South African
5 Italian
6 Austrian
7 Chinese
8 Irish
9 Egyptian
10 Argentinian
11 Greek
12 American
13 German
14 Indian
15 German/Russian

C 1 India   6 Czech
2 Italy   7 Taiwan
3 Ireland   8 Bangladeshi
4 France   9 Brazil
5 Scotland   10 South Korea

Unit 37

A 1 bungalow   4 cellar
2 apartment   5 detached
3 attic

B 1 wardrobe
2 fridge
3 bookshelves
4 television
5 sofa
6 cupboard
7 dishwasher/sink
8 lamp

Unit 38

A 1 Friday, Monday/tomorrow,
Wednesday
2 31st December, New Year's
Eve
3 Christmas, New Year, etc.
4 On New Year's Day

B 1 30.5.97
2 31st January
3 27.3.98
4 17/9/01
5 22.11.84
6 8th December
7 2nd July 1999
8 March 10th/10th March
9 1st April
10 20.2.52

C 1E 2D 3B 4A 5C

Unit 39

A The man is wearing a suit with
a waistcoat, a shirt, a striped
tie and shoes. He's also
wearing glasses.
The woman is wearing a long-
sleeved blouse, a patterned
skirt, earrings and high heels.
The girl is wearing a sweater/
jumper, jeans and boots.
The boy is wearing a (casual)
jacket and jeans, with a T-
shirt/sweatshirt and trainers.

B 1 size   5 fit
2 suits   6 on
3 of   7 wearing
4 goes   8 buttons

Unit 40

A 1 Switzerland
2 Greece
3 France
4 Turkey
5 Italy
6 Argentina
7 the Netherlands
8 Germany
9 Wales
10 Portugal
11 Iceland
12 China
13 Scotland
14 Malta
15 Spain
16 Australia
17 Brazil
18 Austria
19 South Korea
20 India

B 1 May   5 March
2 January   6 September
3 July   7 November
4 February

C *Suggested answers:*
1 They are all worn on the
feet, except *gloves*.
2 A *dress* is worn on the whole
body, while the others are
worn only on feet or legs.
3 They all refer to designs of
material, except *swimsuit*.
4 They are all worn in cold
weather, except *sandals*.
5 They are all materials,
except *waistcoat*.

D 1 You use a *dishwasher* to
wash your dirty dishes.

2 The *freezer* is the best place to keep ice cream and frozen food for a long time.

3 Dinner plates are usually stored in *cupboards* when they are not being used.

4 ✔

5 A *wardrobe* is very useful for hanging your clothes.

Unit 41

A 1 carton   5 can
2 packet   6 jars/pots
3 box   7 tube
4 packet   8 packet

B 1 packet of cereal   1 packet/pound/ kilo of butter
1 bar of chocolate   2 small loaves of brown bread
2 bags/ pounds/kilos of white sugar   a kilo/pound/ piece of cheese
1 tin of chicken soup   1 tube of glue
1 bottle of shampoo   1 bag of flour
1 jar/pot of honey
2 pints/litres/ cartons of milk

Unit 42

A 1C   2D   3A   4E   5B

B 1 game/ match   5 games/ matches
2 beat   6 win
3 score   7 players
4 referee   8 lose

C 1 spare   4 bat
2 collecting   5 give
3 racket

Unit 43

A 1 artist
2 manager/boss
3 plumber/(heating) engineer
4 architect
5 vet
6 journalist
7 engineer
8 factory worker

B 1C   2A   3E   4F   5B   6D

C 1 lawyer   4 plumber
2 electrician   5 taxi driver
3 doctor

Unit 44

A 1C   2A   3E   4B   5D

B 1 camera   5 credit card
2 currency   6 passport
3 sun cream
4 travel insurance

C 1 up   6 set
2 went   7 stayed
3 booked   8 by
4 guidebook   9 time
5 packed

Unit 45

A 1D   2H   3F   4A   5B   6G
7C   8E

B 1 youth hostel   4 villa
2 scheduled   5 guidebook
3 rucksack

C 1B   2A   3D   4C   5B   6D
7A   8C   9B

Unit 46

A 1 A *town* is a large and important group of houses, shops, schools, cinemas, etc.

2 It can be *dangerous* to live close to a volcano.

3 ✔

4 If you go mountain climbing, you *need* special equipment.

5 I *loved* it. It was breathtaking./ I'm afraid not. It was *nothing special*.

B 1 canals   4 mountain
2 villages, lake   5 agricultural
3 forest   6 beach

C 1 mountains   4 city/town
2 valleys   5 banks
3 lakes   6 lake

Unit 47

A 1 love story   6 quiz show
2 chat show   7 ghost story
3 trailer   8 commercial
4 tragedy   9 western/
5 pop/rock   action movie

B 1 special effects   5 ballet
2 cartoons   6 science
3 documentary   fiction
4 quiz show   7 comedy

Unit 48

A 1D   2A   3B   4F   5C   6E

B 1 ear   11 hand
2 eye   12 finger(s)
3 nose   13 thumb
4 mouth   14 waist
5 cheek   15 hip
6 neck   16 leg
7 back   17 knee
8 shoulder   18 ankle
9 elbow   19 foot
10 wrist   20 toe(s)

C 1 leg   6 hands
2 mouth   7 thumb
3 ankle   8 shoulders
4 toes   9 foot
5 knee   10 nose

Unit 49

A 1 lion   4 elephant
2 rhinoceros   5 hamster
3 whale   6 tiger

B 1E   2G   3H   4F   5A   6D
7B   8C

C 1 pet   4 cat
2 dog   5 hamster
3 horse

Unit 50

A 1A   2B   3B   4B   5A   6A
7B   8A

B 1C DIRECTION
2E WATER
3A ANIMALS
4B A HIGH PLACE
5F HOME
6D TREES
7H SAND
8G PEOPLE

C 1D   2C   3B   4A

Unit 51

A 1B   2A   3G   4E   5C   6F
7D

B *Suggested answers:*
1 Cod, because the others are meat.
2 Lettuce, because the others are fruit.
3 Carrots, because the others are green.
4 Bake, because the others are ways of cooking that need water.
5 Tea, because you usually drink it hot.

C 1 'Excuse me, this is very greasy.'
2 'Excuse me, this soup is cold.'
3 'Excuse me, this is undercooked.'
4 'Excuse me, this is much too hot/spicy.'
5 'Excuse me, (I just want to say) this is delicious.'
6 'Excuse me, this fish is dry and tasteless.'

Unit 52
A 1C 2G 3J 4I 5H 6A 7D 8B 9E 10F

B 1 parents
2 relationship
3 niece
4 mother-in-law
5 close

Unit 53
A 1 misty/foggy 4 pouring
2 showery 5 chilly
3 cold/freezing 6 boiling

B 1 drought
2 breeze
3 floods
4 gale/hurricane/storm
5 spell

C 1D 2B 3A 4A 5C 6C
7B 8C 9B 10C 11D
12D 13B 14C

Unit 54
A 1 state 7 uniforms
2 lessons 8 homework
3 pupils 9 passed
4 class 10 course
5 education 11 student
6 private 12 teacher

B 1 courses 5 revise
2 taking 6 pupil
3 teacher 7 homework
4 secondary 8 timetable

Unit 55
A 1 stepmother/mother
2 cousin
3 uncle
4 niece
5 mother-in-law
6 nephew
7 brother-in-law
8 aunt

B 1 snow 5 hot
2 rain 6 drought
3 rain 7 wet
4 gale 8 freezing

C 1C 2A 3B 4D 5B 6A
7C 8D 9B 10A

Unit 56
A 1E 2C 3F 4A 5B 6D

B 1 How do you do?
2 Pleased to meet you.
3 What's your name?
4 Hello there, fancy seeing you again!
5 Jill, have you met my cousin?
6 Sorry, do I know you?
7 I think we've met before.
8 I'll be in touch.
9 See you later.
10 See you soon/Keep in touch.

Unit 57
A 1 name 7 at
2 from 8 single
3 speaks 9 hobbies
4 a 10 the
5 unemployed 11 the
6 in 12 travelling/going

B 1 caravan 5 an
2 divorced 6 supporting
3 from 7 in
4 speaks 8 unemployed

Unit 58
A 1 did 4 have
2 does 5 didn't
3 were

B 1 will 6 can
2 hasn't 7 is
3 couldn't 8 doesn't
4 isn't 9 don't
5 did 10 aren't

C 1 So where exactly do you live?
2 How many brothers and sisters have you got?
3 How do you come to school or work?
4 How long does it take?
5 Where do you have lunch?
6 What do you have for breakfast, lunch and dinner?
7 What are your hobbies?
8 Where do you go for your holidays every year?
9 What kind of music, films and books do you like best?
10 What subjects do you like studying, talking about or writing about?

Unit 59
A 1 Does this mean I can't park here? What's a voucher?
2 Does this mean I can/can't go in? I'm not a member.
3 What does this mean?
4 Does this mean children must pay more, or they can't go in?
5 Does this mean twelve things to pay for?
6 What must we do with our dogs?

B *Suggested answers:*
1 Sorry, what was that?
2 I'm not sure what 'zigzag' means.
3 What's the Heimlich manoeuvre? Can you explain it?
4 What does that/'sudden death' mean?
5 Sorry, what were their names? What do you mean exactly?

6 Right, I'll do all that every
night, shall I?/You're saying
you want me to switch off
the photocopier, switch on
the answerphone, and set
the security alarm before
I leave every night.

7 What do you mean?/I don't
follow.

Unit 60

A *Possible answers:*
1 (From the tourist office) Go
down here past the library
and turn left into Spring
Street. Carry on over the
crossroads and you'll see a
chemist on your left, just
past the traffic lights.

2 (From the library) Go up this
street, past the tourist office
on the right, and turn into
the first street on your right.
Turn right again at the end,
into Station Road, and then
take the first left, into
Theatre Street. The theatre
is a bit further on on the left,
at the end of the street.

3 (From outside the chemist on
Westgate Street) Go straight
up here, and over the bridge.
You'll see the Health Centre
on the other side of the river,
on your right, just before you
get to Queen's Avenue. You
can't miss it.

4 (From the department store)
Turn right as you leave the
store, and go up to the big
roundabout. Take the
second exit, which is
Westgate Street. The library
is on the left at the end,
where Westgate Street joins
Spring Street.

5 (From the theatre) Let me
think – it's on the corner of
Tennis Lane and Green
Street. The best way to go is
along this street to the end,
and then turn right into
Wells Road. At the traffic
lights, turn left into Tennis
Lane and keep going until
you see the supermarket on
your left.

6 (From the railway station)
There's one on Spring
Street. Turn left out of the
station, then right at the
traffic lights. Just before the
next lights, you'll see a bank
on your left, opposite the
bus station. It's not far.

B 1 1) Excuse 2) way
3) think/see 4) straight
5) turning/road 6) far
7) miss

2 1) this 2) station 3) idea
4) stranger

3 1) somewhere/anywhere
2) further 3) corner

C 1 side   4 suitable
2 the   5 left
3 Me   6 to

D 1 get   6 reach
2 way   7 along
3 tell   8 turn
4 nearest   9 further
5 past

Unit 61

A 1K 2J 3G 4A 5H 6D
7B 8E 9F 10I 11L 12C

B 1b 2a 3b 4c 5a 6c

C 1C 2E 3D 4F 5B 6G
7A

D 1F, on a road
2T, in a shopping centre
3F, in the countryside
4F, outside public toilets
5F, in a supermarket
6T, in the countryside or in a
car park
7F, in a café or restaurant
8T, at an airport or seaport

Unit 62

A 1F 2D 3E 4A 5C 6B

B 1 of
2 wonderful/fantastic/
brilliant
3 much
4 awful/boring
5 much
6 wonderful/fantastic/
brilliant
7 boring
8 best

Unit 63

A 1G 2E 3D 4A 5H 6C
7F 8B

B 1 cost   4 map
2 timetable   5 far away
3 dangerous   6 ferry

C *Suggested answers:*
1 Could you help me, please?
I'd like to find somewhere to
stay here. I'd like do some
sightseeing and other
activities.
2 Have you any free leaflets?
3 Are the beaches safe for
swimming?

Unit 64

A 1 stamp   4 weigh
2 1st   5 registered post
3 parcel   6 (customs) form

B 1 It's quicker.
2 To get some money back if
something valuable is lost.
3 To weigh it.
4 A customs form.

C 1C 2D 3A 4E 5F 6B

D *Suggested answers:*
1 It's going abroad, to
Sweden.
2 1st class, please.
3 Yes, I opened one last
month.
4 I'd like a statement every
month.

Unit 65

A 1 menu
2 aperitif
3 meal/dinner/lunch
4 starter
5 soup
6 main
7 vegetables
8 dessert
9 wine

B 1 book   5 check
2 double   6 half
3 private   7 credit
4 view   8 confirm

Unit 66

A Bus: 3, 4
Train: 1, 2, 5, 8, 10
Both: 6, 7, 9, 11, 12

B 1 fare   4 driver
2 stop   5 running
3 bus   6 carriages

C *Suggested answers:*
1 Could I have a day return to London, please?
2 Can I smoke on the train?
3 Does this bus go to Redhill station?
4 Is this seat for the elderly or disabled?
5 Which platform for the train to Exeter, please?
6 I'd like a season ticket, please.

Unit 67

A 1D   2F   3G   4H   5B   6A
7E   8C

B 1 speak   4 message
2 sorry   5 call/ring/phone
3 moment

C 1 ✔
2 operator: a person who connects calls
3 to dial: to call a number by pressing buttons or turning a dial
4 ✔
5 ✔

Unit 68

A 1 try   4 bargain
2 fitting   5 sale
3 size

B 1 supermarket   4 carrier bag
2 on   5 second-hand
3 checkout   6 stock

C *Suggested answers:*
1 No thanks, I'm just looking.
2 Could I try these on, please?
3 Can I pay by credit card?
4 and 5 *Subjective answers*

Unit 69

A 1 turn   4 dial, clockwise
2 added, is   5 pulling, turn
3 press

B 1 switch   5 dial
2 card   6 put
3 press   7 slot
4 on   8 button

C *Suggested answers:*
1 Shall I switch it on?
2 Try plugging it in!
3 Seats are made in Spain.
4 I usually turn everything off.

Unit 70

A 1A   2U   3D   4A (with Michelle)   5D   6A   7D   8U   9U

Unit 71

A 1D   2G   3E   4H   5F   6C
7A   8B

B *Suggested answers:*
1 Thank you for having me/looking after me.
2 I'm so sorry, it was an accident.
3 I do apologise. I didn't mean to do it.
4 Thanks very much/How kind of you!
5 Thanks very much. I *am* grateful.
6 I'm awfully sorry (to the driver). I'm terribly sorry. It won't happen again, I promise (to your father).
7 Thanks very much indeed.
8 I'm so sorry, I forgot to ring you.

Unit 72

A 1B   2C   3F   4E   5D   6A

B *Suggested answers:*
1 Could I borrow your hairdryer?
2 Could I possibly have supper early?
3 May I borrow your book?
4 May I leave class early to go to the dentist?
5 Would it be all right if I went home now?
6 Could I have a vegetarian meal?
7 Can I borrow your bike for a few minutes?

8 No, I'm afraid you can't/I'd rather you didn't.
9 Not at all, please do.
10 No, I'm afraid you can't.

Unit 73

A 1B   2C   3B   4A   5C   6C
7A

B 1 tell   6 ask
2 go   7 watching
3 have   8 get
4 take   9 eating
5 buying   10 try

C *Suggested answers:*
1 Why don't you ask your parents for some?
2 How about trying to mend it yourself?
3 We could visit the castle and go for a swim.
4 Let's go skiing.

Unit 74

A 1E   2D   3A   4B   5C

B c, f, a, d, g, b, e

C 1 way
2 news
3 break/butt
4 Excuse

D *Possible answers:*
1 Excuse me/Sorry, could you help me?/can/could you explain how this works?
2 By the way, what about our party?/what about the party we're planning to give?
3 Sorry to break in, but this is delicious!/That reminds me, I'll have to buy a new mobile …

Unit 75

A 1 Will   6 I'd
2 like   7 unable
3 sorry   8 fun
4 to   9 lovely
5 look   10 you to go

B *Suggested answers:*
1 Can you all come to my party?
2 I'd love to. What fun!
3 Oh, I *am* sorry. I won't be able to.

4 Would you like to have dinner with me and my family?

5 Sorry, I can't make it.

6 I'd be delighted to accept./ Yes, that would be lovely.

Unit 76

A 1 or 6 were
2 out 7 advice
3 ought 8 better
4 I'll 9 don't
5 should 10 careful

B *Suggested answers:*

1 You'd better tell her about it.

2 If I were you, I wouldn't worry.

3 You ought to start studying now.

4 I think you should stay at home more, and spend some time on homework, or you'll fail your exams.

5 Be careful! The floor is very wet.

6 You'll lose your friends if you don't start telling the truth.

7 You'd better go home to bed.

8 Watch out! You'll hit your head.

Unit 77

A 1 return 5 replacement
2 wrong 6 refund
3 seem 7 manager
4 receipt

B *Suggested answers:*

1 The television I bought isn't working.

2 I'm not happy with the food we've just eaten. It was terrible!

3 There's something wrong with these photos.

4 I refuse to pay until my hair's the right colour.

5 I'm afraid this fish is bad. I'd like a refund, please.

6 I'm not happy with the service here.

7 The whole holiday was awful. I'd like a refund, and you should pay me compensation, too.

8 Could you replace this, please, as several pages are missing? Here's my receipt.

Unit 78

A Some years ago, in the month of June, two men arrived at the North Pole. Their names were Professor Donald Shawcross and Doctor Jeff Thomas. For twelve days they had walked across a thousand miles of ice, carrying or pulling all their food and equipment. They were both Canadian, and had done their training in Alaska and the Rocky Mountains.

B 1 friend 6 chief
2 receive 7 receipt
3 believe 8 deceive
4 thief 9 field
5 niece 10 ceiling

C 1 potatoes 7 families
2 children 8 heroes
3 feet 9 knives
4 sheep 10 fish
5 buses 11 mice
6 wolves 12 women

D 1 running 9 clapping
2 ✔ 10 ✔
3 waving 11 ✔
4 becoming 12 dripping
5 getting 13 bigger
6 ✔ 14 ✔
7 ✔ 15 ✔
8 ✔ 16 shopping

E their/there, princes/princess, casle/castle, beautifull/beautiful, heir/hair, know/no, freinds/friends, wen/when, riting/writing, heared/heard, hansome/handsome, hoarse/horse, four/for, Your/You're, to/too, beleive/believe, cuboard/cupboard, nife/knife, climed/climbed, Hear/Here, no/know

F 1 advertisement
2 accommodation
3 beginning

4 stories (or storeys = floors)
5 comfortable
6 sadder
7 necessary
8 ✔
9 ✔
10 journey
11 really
12 ✔
13 business
14 police
15 holiday
16 mistake
17 apartment
18 college
19 ✔
20 except

Unit 79

A GOOD: super, wonderful, exciting, great, excellent, delicious, busy(?)

BAD: terrible, awful, crowded, miserable, disgusting, changeable, busy(?), cold, noisy, unpleasant

B 1 cloudy 9 thundery
2 foggy 10 windy
3 frosty 11 frosty
4 icy 12 foggy
5 misty 13 rainy
6 rainy 14 sunny
7 snowy 15 thundery
8 sunny

C 1 Highways Agency, 890 – 898 Southwick Street, London SE1 0TE

2 Paul Holmes, 12 Church Street, Exmouth EX8 3TS

3 Barbara Wilson, Flat 7, Sillwood House, Sillwood Street, Brighton BN1 7BC

4 Edward Canham, 72 Lindfield Close, Oxford OX3 8PR

5 Ahmed Hadi, 20 Mayborn Way, Edinburgh EH5 1SA Scotland

6 Tony Griffiths, 196 Woodland Drive, Shrewsbury SY2 3AB

7 Jane Campbell, 25 North Road, York, Yorkshire Y01 8TG

8 Ken Lambert, 6A West
   Avenue, Aylesbury
   HP20 5BP

D Dear *(name)*, This is *a*
beautiful place. I *am* very
happy here. The sun *shines*
every day. Yesterday I *went* to
see the king's palace. *How* are
you? Maybe next year we'*ll*
have *a* holiday together. Write
to me soon. Best *wishes,* Georg

  Address: *20 Duke Street,
  Oxford OX2 8ES*

Unit 80

A 1T (probably) 2F 3F 4F

B b, d, f, a, c, e

C 1 Dear Mum and Dad,
   2 May come and visit this
      weekend
   3 if we can borrow a car.
   4 Is that OK?
   5 Love, Jane

D 1 buy/get, pay
   2 hear, soon, when
   3 bike, need, old, condition

Unit 81

A 1E 2A 3J 4C 5I 6H
   7B 8F 9D 10G

B *Possible answers:*
Answers should be in block
capitals. Boxes should have
ticks (not crosses).
First name: ANGELA
Surname: HAMPTON
Title: MISS/MS
Initials: A. H.
Sex: Female ✔
Marital status: SINGLE
Age: 24
Height: 1.60 m
Occupation: STUDENT
Nationality: CANADIAN
Country of birth: CANADA
Place of birth: TORONTO
Address: 10 HAWKHURST
ROAD, LONDON
Postcode: NE20 3TS
Signature: *Angela Hampton*
Date: today's date

Unit 82

A 1 until   6 but
   2 during   7 as soon as
   3 for   8 because
   4 in order to 9 Although
   5 so   10 Either

B 1 such   5 so
   2 so   6 so
   3 such   7 such
   4 such   8 such

C 1 where C   5 but B
   2 because F 6 that G
   3 while A   7 so E
   4 until H   8 in order to D

D 1 where   6 that
   2 and   7 While
   3 until   8 although
   4 So   9 or
   5 because 10 but

E 1 Although I put some sun
      cream on, I still got burnt!
   2 James learnt a lot during his
      stay in Uganda.
   3 It was such a boring
      programme that Gavin fell
      asleep.
   4 Daniela went to Kyoto to
      buy some presents.
   5 They could either say
      yes/Either they could say
      yes, or they could say no.
   6 Write to me soon, so (that) I
      can book the tickets.
   7 She saved a lot of money,
      but she couldn't afford to go
      on holiday.
   8 I'll ring him back when/as
      soon as I get home.
   9 He asked her to marry him,
      because he loved her.
   10 Fiona had a shower before
      she went to bed.
   11 Janie had a headache, so she
      took an aspirin.
   12 They were such kind people
      that we felt at home.

Unit 83

A 1 I would like to ask for more
      information.
   2 I am not happy with the
      service I received.
   3 I would like to apply for the
      post of ...
   4 We would like to invite you
      to a coffee morning.
   5 I look forward to receiving
      your reply/hearing from you
      soon.

B f, b, i, c, g, j, d, k, l, e, a, h

C I look forward to ..., I apologize
for ..., I would like to apply ...,
Could you tell me ..., Yours
faithfully, Dear Madam,

Unit 84

A f, b, h, c, i, e, g, d, j, a

B 1 I'm sorry
   2 How are you
   3 guess what happened
   4 Do you remember
   5 I don't know why
   6 Isn't it fantastic
   7 It's really nice
   8 if you like
   9 How about
   10 for ages
   11 let me know
   12 Best wishes

Unit 85

Subjective answers

Unit 86

A 1 took   11 sank
   2 drove   12 taught, knew
   3 understood 13 shook, met
   4 gave   14 fell
   5 kept   15 forgot
   6 woke   16 went
   7 swam   17 lost
   8 sold   18 made
   9 rode   19 chose
   10 saw   20 became

B g, a, j, c, f, b, i, d, h, e

C 1 suddenly
   2 As soon as
   3 then
   4 Unfortunately
   5 before
   6 as
   7 After
   8 at last

Unit 87

A
1 Went to Athens for important meeting.
2 Pam forgot to close back door, so cat got in.
3 Arrived at bank – closed, so couldn't pay in cheque.
4 Dimitri drove to airport to meet grandmother.
5 Hope our team will win match.
6 Rita told me to apply for job in Export Department.
7 Book I wanted not available.
8 Great party – had super time.
9 Remember – go to library and do shopping.
10 Invited all my friends to barbecue.

B *Suggested answers:*
SUNDAY Flew to Amsterdam to meet Heidi. Had birthday lunch in super restaurant. Stayed night at Heidi's house.

MONDAY Flew to Florence. Meeting with manager of Adidas 4 p.m. Staying at Atlantic Hotel. Very tired, so went to bed early.

TUESDAY Went to Uffizi. Lunch in café. Plane back to London 3 p.m.

WEDNESDAY In office all day. Wrote reports and had meetings with J. B. Tennis with Alex 6.30 p.m. Great fun! Played really well.

THURSDAY To Oxford by train to see Mr Hansen about his Ranger jeans. Took me to French restaurant for lunch (delicious food!). But dropped door key under table (?). Had to break kitchen window to get in to flat! Police came – had to explain! Awful!

FRIDAY Quiet day in office. Watched news and film in evening.

SATURDAY Shopping. Bought two great pairs of shoes. Very expensive! Bought some food and invited Ted, Susie and Jeremy round to dinner. Meal was huge success! Stayed up late listening to music.

Unit 88

A It was so nice to get your letter. I've been wanting to write to you for a long time, but you know I'm very lazy!

I'm glad you're enjoying your new job. It's fun, isn't it? Since I saw you last I've been doing lots of different things. First I travelled to Rome to meet my friend, then we went to the south of Italy to pick grapes. It was hard work, but the pay was good. After three months I came back home to go on studying at university. Now I'm looking forward to the holidays next year!

Can you come to visit me? There's lots of room for you to sleep on my floor! Write and tell me soon.

Best wishes,
Daniel

B
1 *I've lived/been living* near the city centre since I arrived *in* Kyoto.
2 Andy *washes* the dishes every evening after supper.
3 All the people in the office *were* working *hard* that day.
4 We could go to *the* cinema if there is *a* good film on.
5 I think everybody *likes* the new Italian restaurant.
6 Keith *forgot* his umbrella, so he got wet.
7 Your hair looks great! *Did you have it cut* yesterday?
8 The old man was wearing *(a pair of)* very dirty *trousers*.
9 The police *were* very *grateful* for the *information*.
10 Fritz *(had)* studied hard, but *failed* the exam.
11 The television news *was* not very *interesting* today.
12 Although *it was* raining, we went shopping anyway.

C
1A men, children, teeth, feet, beaches, leaves, tomatoes
1B thief, running, ponies, climbing, knee, helpful
2A informal
2B Regards/Yours
3A Yes, if you're e-mailing a friend.
3B Your name or initials
4A teacher, housewife, student, doctor
4B single, married, divorced, widowed
5A during, while
5B such a big dog
6A Yours sincerely
6B Dear James
7A tall, thin, slim, fat, plump etc.
7B sociable, polite, selfish, kind, mean, etc.
8A past continuous, past simple, past perfect
8B Yes, you do.
9A It helps you to think in English.
9B You use short sentences, note form, conversational English, short forms, exclamations, sometimes no subject pronoun or articles.